REFUGEE

A MEMOIR

REVISED AND UPDATED WITH NEW CHAPTERS BY THE AUTHOR

TRANSLATED BY CHARLOTTE COLLINS
FROM THE GERMAN TRANSLATION BY ALEXANDER BEHR

FARRAR, STRAUS AND GIROUX | NEW YORK

REFUGEE

EMMANUEL MBOLELA

Farrar, Straus and Giroux
120 Broadway, New York 10271

Printed in the United States of America
Originally published in German in 2014 by Mandelbaum Verlag, Germany, as
Mein Weg vom Kongo nach Europa
English translation published in the United States by Farrar, Straus and Giroux
First American edition, 2021

Library of Congress Cataloging-in-Publication Data
Names: Mbolela, Emmanuel, 1973– author. | Collins, Charlotte, 1967–
translator.
Title: Refugee : a memoir / Emmanuel Mbolela ; translated by
Charlotte Collins from the German translation by Alexander Behr ;
revised and updated with new chapters by the author.
Other titles: Mein Weg vom Kongo nach Europa. English.
Description: First American edition. | New York : Farrar, Straus and Giroux,
2021. | "Originally published in German in 2014 by Mandelbaum Verlag,
Germany, as Mein Weg vom Kongo nach Europa." | Summary: "A memoir
of a Congolese political refugee's harrowing six-year journey from the
DRC to the Netherlands"— Provided by publisher.
Identifiers: LCCN 2020052552 | ISBN 9780374240929 (hardcover)
Subjects: LCSH: Mbolela, Emmanuel, 1973– | Political refugees—Congo
(Democratic Republic)—Biography. | Congo (Democratic Republic)—
Politics and government—1997–
Classification: LCC DT658.2.M39 A3 2021 | DDC 967.5103/4092 [B]—dc23
LC record available at https://lccn.loc.gov/2020052552

Designed by Abby Kagan

Our books may be purchased in bulk for promotional, educational, or business
use. Please contact your local bookseller or the Macmillan Corporate and
Premium Sales Department at 1-800-221-7945, extension 5442, or by email at
MacmillanSpecialMarkets@macmillan.com.

www.fsgbooks.com
www.twitter.com/fsgbooks • www.facebook.com/fsgbooks

1   3   5   7   9   10   8   6   4   2

CONTENTS

R eading the English edition of this remarkable book reminded me of something an aunt said to me years ago: a metaphor for tackling life's more daunting challenges. "Remember what it's like after you host a large gathering," she said. "Everyone's left, and you're exhausted, but you still have to clear away the mess. You can't think where to begin. Then, out of the corner of your eye, you notice an ashtray right beside your hand. You drop your fingers, pick it up, flick your wrist, and empty the contents into a bin. That's followed by the leftovers on a plate alongside; and so the cleanup begins, each movement following on from the next, until at last the room is tidy." Everything, she said, starts with a small, often barely perceptible step.

Emmanuel Mbolela's decision to establish ARCOM, a not-for-profit organization assisting Congolese asylum seekers, in Morocco in 2005—when, as a migrant of irregular status, he, too, was vulnerable to deportation—was his subtle yet transformative step forward.

Emmanuel's story begins in Mbuji-Mayi in the 1980s, in

what is now the Democratic Republic of the Congo (the DRC). As a student, Emmanuel's exposure to the injustices of authoritarian rule stirred him to oppose state repression, and the price he paid for his early activism was terribly high. Imprisoned, tortured, he knew he was no longer safe in the country of his birth. Like so many others in the political opposition, once released, he left his family and friends in search of a place where he might have a future, somewhere freedom and justice were respected.

His journey through Africa and eventual arrival in Europe are vividly portrayed, with wrenching descriptions of the immense pain suffered by migrants, of their commitment to their families, and their fight for survival. His book also reveals the cruelties of the criminally minded, the insensitivity of far too many governments and their bureaucrats, and the xenophobia, the racism, the sexual and gender-based violence inflicted on migrants—the extent of which is still largely unknown to far too many people in the Western world. Importantly, Emmanuel also pays tribute to the kindness and selflessness of many others, to whom we all owe a debt of gratitude.

Emmanuel's suffering while in transit and while living as a sans-papiers (undocumented migrant) dampened his spirit at times, but he never lost his thoughtfulness and desire to help others whenever he could. In the four years he lived in Morocco, he set up small but important health care and schooling initiatives for the migrant community—a preparation for the founding of ARCOM, which thrust him into a different league.

He had good reason to be nervous about taking such a step, given his perilous circumstances, but felt that he had no choice. It was courageous, because he knew full well that it would instantly make him more visible to the Moroccan police at a time when visibility was synonymous with deportation. Yet it was also a masterstroke. By dedicating himself to the protection of the wider community, and achieving some crucial early successes, Emmanuel was able not only to protect himself better but also to unlock a profound sense of personal mission. His destination was no longer defined simply by geography—reaching Europe— but by the embracing and active promotion of universal human rights. Refusing to be merely a long-suffering victim of circumstance, he took his fate and that of his community into his own hands, becoming a leader who fashioned his own circumstances.

For anyone who feels similarly helpless, this book is a study in the art of taking control, intelligently, step by step, whatever the odds, and reshaping fate by investing in others, particularly in grassroots networks.

ARCOM was geared to settling practical issues, but it also asked more profound questions. How do we square Africa's vast resources with its continued state of impoverishment? What is the current relationship between the commodities markets and the persistence of despotic rule in Africa? How does one make sense of these conditions, in the context of Europe's position on immigration? Is it not the case, Emmanuel asks, that all human beings, including migrants, are entitled to protection, whatever their legal status? How can the simple fact of being a migrant mean that you are a criminal? He is right on both counts. In 2014, my office, the Office of the United Nations High Commissioner for Human Rights, issued a document, "Principles and Guidelines on Human Rights at International Borders," which set out how all migrants, irrespective of legal status, ought to be treated. The principles included the centrality of human rights in all border governance issues; that migrants should be protected against any form of discrimination at borders; and that states should consider the individual circumstances of all migrants at borders. It is to my profound regret that, six years on, the implementation of this guidance remains a work in progress. The struggle continues.

Emmanuel's odyssey echoes the central theme of Farid ud-Din Attar's twelfth-century epic poem, *The Conference of the Birds*: that of the journey and the destination becoming one. This book restores our faith in action, and in the almost miraculous possibilities that arise when action is directed to the service of others. We should all take careful note of this, and be grateful to Emmanuel Mbolela for his example.

—Zeid Ra'ad Al Hussein, UN High Commissioner
for Human Rights, 2014–2018
New York, April 2020

PREFACE TO THE ENGLISH EDITION

They wanted to silence me. They didn't know that I was a messenger.

Prison is one of the weapons African dictators use to silence those who oppose their nontransparent ways of governing their countries. I did not escape this weapon in my own country, the so-called Democratic Republic of the Congo. For organizing and participating in a peaceful demonstration, I was thrown into prison, where I endured extreme physical and mental torture. Forced to leave my country, I suffered many more acts of violence on my journey into exile: racketeering by customs officers, the trade of human trafficking, being ambushed in the Sahara desert, working illegally in Tamanrasset to finance the rest of the journey, and, finally, the trap of Morocco, where I remained stuck for four years before I finally came to the Netherlands in 2008. Here I went on to write this book, which has become an instrument in this fight and allows me to give voice to the voiceless.

My book was first published in German in June 2014. It appeared in French in January 2016, and in Italian in 2018. I have been getting into and out of planes, trains, buses, and cars ever since, meeting people all over Europe. I have facilitated more than four hundred conferences in high schools and universities, libraries and bookshops, institutions and organizations, theaters and collectives, in villages, in the countryside, in farms and cities, in numerous European countries—Austria, Belgium, France, Germany, Italy, Luxembourg, the Netherlands, Portugal, Spain, Switzerland. These conferences have allowed me, on the one hand, to talk about my journey, about the fundamental issues that forced me, and hundreds of thousands like me, to embark on this odyssey, and about my commitment to the fight in defense of migrants and their cause. On the other hand, and especially, these encounters with people from all socio-professional categories have helped me to listen, in order to understand what grassroots Europe knew of these issues, and what impression they had formed of Africans' migration. I have met people who have not remained indifferent to the cause I defend. This cause, first and foremost my own, is also that of thousands who, like me, have been forced to leave their countries, impelled by the various reasons that the reader will learn about in this book. Many of those who have listened to my lectures or read my book have committed themselves to playing their part in this fight— the fight against the war on migrants. I recall the banner held aloft by students in the audience at the University of Vienna: "They are here because we were there."

These human beings have been denied their humanity. Our only crime is to have taken the path that leads to Europe. Migrants who manage to escape death in the desert are stranded in North African countries like Morocco and Libya, where they endure cruel and degrading treatment; meanwhile, those who manage to cross the Mediterranean and reach European soil are taken to detention centers where they are subjected to indescribable physical and psychological violence before being deported back to their countries of origin.

The sad conditions of migrants from sub-Saharan Africa were exposed to the world in a CNN report on the trafficking of migrants in Libya. The decision makers of this world professed to be surprised by the report's revelations of people subjugated and sold in Libyan slave markets. Yet it is the consequence of their discriminatory and xenophobic migration policies, the walls and border controls they are constantly putting in place, and their cooperation with Libyan militias over border control, which allows victims to be controlled by the very people who are persecuting them. The anger those horrendous images provoked quickly faded. Yet this odious practice—which recalls the fate endured by our grandparents and great-grandparents, dehumanized and uprooted from their countries of origin to be sold as slaves—is carried out with the complicity of the member states of the European Union, which nonetheless claims to be a guarantor of the protection of human rights.

I am writing the preface to the English edition of this book while on a conference tour in Italy, Libya's neighbor. Here, migrants refuse to be defeated by humiliation; they struggle on a daily basis for survival. They do not remain idle. They fight on, in the hope that one day they will regain their dignity. I came to meet with them. I told them about my journey, which was similar to theirs. They told me about the difficulties they face. They live in a state of uncertainty. They are called illegals, "clandestines," although they are not hidden away. They walk the streets and spend their nights in stations, public parks, or on the sidewalk. They want residence permits, which are essential if they are to rebuild their lives and find work. But the key to this door is denied them; they are trapped, forced to live in limbo, as I was in Morocco. Just before the conference in Verona, I spoke to a young man who told me he was sold as a slave in Libya: "I was made to work very hard, in inhumane conditions. I endured physical torture. When I saw a chance, I ran away and took a small boat, and reached Italy, thank God, where I'm coping with a new stage of suffering. But I hope that all this will be consigned to history while I am still alive."

Courage is born of necessity, they say. Yes: we left because we had no alternative. As a woman I spoke to at our women's shelter said: "In my country, after studying, I got married and had children, then suddenly my husband and I were out of work. I couldn't even buy my own children a piece of bread. That's why I decided to leave. I entrusted my children to my mother and told them, 'I'm going in search of your dignity.' For my part, as I didn't die in the desert, it may be that I die in the sea, but at least my children will know that their mother died because she left to fight for them. And if ever I manage to cross the sea and reach Europe, I will work hard to give my children dignity. The worst thing for me would be to stay in my country and have to look my children in the eye. I cannot bear to see my children suffer while I, their mother, am alive."

Europe, where people are heading in search of dignity for themselves and for their families, is barricading itself in. Its borders are hermetically sealed. Walls are being built from east to west, from north to south. Agreements imposed on some African countries require them to control their borders and repel what is referred to as "illegal immigration." In the name of protecting its borders, Europe is letting migrants die in the Mediterranean, on the pretext that saving them would create an incentive. These human beings have no name and no country. They are all dubbed "illegal." For a long time they were simply abandoned to feed the fish; now they are handed over to lawless Libyan militias. Their lives have no value; their deaths no longer provoke any emotion.

The Mediterranean has become the mass grave of thousands of migrants, Libya the marketplace where migrants are transformed into twenty-first-century slaves. This isn't happening the way it does in the desert, far from television cameras and journalists, but in full view of the whole world. Bodies are found and buried with no attempt made to find the families and alert them. Nor are any efforts made to free those held hostage by Libyan militias; there are only outward expressions of emotion. Instead, what we see is the remarkable, complicit silence of those in power in both Africa and Europe. We are witnessing a cooperation between European countries and the Libyan militias who are being paid to lock up migrants and inflict cruel and inhumane treatment upon them.

I am one of these people. On my journey to Europe, I, like so many other migrants, was robbed by bandits in the desert, had to work in the black economy in Tamanrasset; I had to hide for months in Algiers, then covertly cross the Algerian border to Morocco, where I was stuck for four long years. My comrades and I fought for our rights. I wrote this book in order to tell our story. I am proud that it has now been translated into and published in English. It will enable me to organize meetings in English-speaking countries, and to broaden my outreach as I continue to raise awareness about these issues.

REFUGEE

INTRODUCTION

I have seen, with my own eyes, my homeland, the Democratic Republic of the Congo (DRC), descend into chaos—a chaos created by dictatorship and neocolonial dependency. It has resulted in human rights abuses, social injustice, and a lack of educational opportunities, not to mention hunger and misery. All these have been aggravated by a senseless war in which millions of my countrymen and -women have lost, and are still losing, their lives.

If I had remained silent in the face of this, I would have felt guilty. So I became an activist while studying for my degree at the University of Mbuji-Mayi in central DRC. I got involved with political organizations and fought, by peaceful means, for a society based on the fundamental values of justice, democracy, and freedom. A few years later, as a consequence of this fight, I was compelled to set off on my journey into exile.

I did not, therefore, leave my country of my own free will. Rather, I left not knowing where I was to go. My main objective was to save my life—an objective that was very nearly thwarted along the way. And yet, thank God, I am still alive.

From my hometown of Mbuji-Mayi I set out for Kinshasa, the capital of the Democratic Republic of the Congo. I traveled on to Brazzaville, Cameroon, Nigeria, Benin, Burkina Faso, Mali, Algeria, and Morocco, before finally reaching the Netherlands.

My aim in writing this book is to share what I experienced along the way in those six years—two spent on the road, and almost four in Morocco, where I was prevented from continuing my journey. Instead of being given asylum there, I was denied any form of protection. The externalization of the European Union's border regime left me stuck there, in a country supposedly governed by peace, law, and order. Like so many other migrants, I was forced to lead a life of inactivity. There was no possibility whatsoever for me to utilize the commodities and infrastructure around me. In these circumstances, nonetheless, I resumed the fight by founding an organization—ARCOM, the Association of Congolese Refugees and Asylum Seekers in Morocco—with which we could defend our rights and freedoms. Through this organization, I helped spearhead the struggle for almost four years, after which the office of the United Nations High Commissioner for Refugees (UNHCR) managed to find a country that would give me asylum. Toward the end of this book, I report on my life in European exile.

As well as undergoing my own trials along the journey into exile, I also heard a great many other people's stories. I wish to recount not only what happened to me along the way, but also the stories I documented during my time as head of ARCOM. In this way, I want to bear witness to what I have seen, experienced, and heard during my time in exile.

My written record of this long and difficult journey is dedicated to the generations to come who will be forced, perhaps for different reasons, to take a similar path to mine. I left behind loved ones, some of whom I will never see again. This book is an outcry on behalf of all the women, men, and especially children I met along the way—children without a voice. Many were subjected to appalling atrocities that cannot be expressed in words in any language. I have seen people raped, tortured, and abandoned. I have seen some of them die. I have seen people wandering in despair, no longer knowing to what god they should pray.

However, I have also seen how men and women of good will could be galvanized into action—including citizens of those countries where order, justice, and, above all, peace exist. These are values we need everywhere, so that those who are compelled to leave their countries are not forced to take the same agonizing route I was. They ought to be spared this experience. Never again!

This book consists of seven chapters. The first introduces the reader to my homeland, the Democratic Republic of the Congo. The second chapter deals with my work and activities before I had to flee. I also explain that my homeland is very large and full of riches, yet its people are forced to live in extreme poverty. This observation leads to a description of the context for my political struggle. In the third chapter, I trace my route from the DRC to Morocco, including an account of how I crossed Algeria and the Sahara. The fourth chapter is devoted to life as an exile in Morocco, where I spent almost four years. The inhumane living conditions in this country compelled me to establish a structure for helping men and women in exile to organize and demand their rights and freedoms. In the fifth chapter, I describe how I set up ARCOM, one of the first organizations ever founded in Morocco by refugees, asylum seekers, and sub-Saharan migrants. The sixth chapter examines in more detail the campaigns and projects we initiated within the ARCOM framework. Finally, chapter 7 deals with life in European exile—caught between hope and reality.

1

THE DEMOCRATIC REPUBLIC OF THE CONGO

The so-called "Democratic" Republic of the Congo—"La République Démocratique du Congo," or the DRC for short—is my homeland. In 2002 I was forced to leave my country as a consequence of my fight to change the dictatorial system there. My comrades and I engaged in this fight with conviction and determination. When I left my country, I left comrades in prison, where they continued to endure physical and mental torture. Others, whom I had seen for the last time, were dead. But our fight was noble and just. Back then, we continued to hope that no matter how hard it would be, no matter what suffering was required of us or how long it might take, we would ultimately be assured of victory, and our hope for that victory was expressed in the slogan of our party: "Keep holding on—the UDPS will be victorious."

At last, in December 2018, elections were held, and Félix Tshisekedi, one of the leaders of our party, was elected the new leader of the DRC. For me and all my comrades, this victory was a major achievement, after all our long years of struggle. As I revise the English version of this book, there are signs of hope.

But the overall situation remains highly ambivalent. Some of my imprisoned friends who managed to survive the oppression and torture of the Kabila regime have now regained their freedom. I visited my country in the summer of 2019 to see with my own eyes the changes that were taking place, and was pleasantly surprised to see people demonstrating in the streets without being bothered by the police—unlike what we experienced in the past.

At the same time, it is obvious that Joseph Kabila and his clique still exert considerable influence. It is clear to everyone that the army, the police, and the security services are not controlled by the new president. Kabilists are also still present in the various sectors of the country's economy. In addition, the former dignitaries have acquired a majority in the parliament and the senate, and the police still arrest and detain peaceful demonstrators. Although I believe that the 2018 election was a huge step forward in the history of my country, it is imperative that we are not blind to the shortcomings of the new government.

In order to understand where we are now, it makes sense to begin with a short introduction to my country, to provide some background to what I will go on to report. I am well aware that this historical section, in particular, may demand a certain amount of effort from readers unfamiliar with the region—first, because since 1994 the DRC has been convulsed by four wars, resulting in many millions of deaths. Second, because those wars can only be properly understood in the context of the 1994 genocide of the Tutsi in the DRC's eastern neighbor, Rwanda. Nonetheless, I don't think anyone in the West should be allowed to take the position that the history of Africa is always complex, violent, and somehow incomprehensible: that is a racist stereotype. The prerequisite for a true decolonialization of the mind is to take an active and differentiated approach to the history of individual African countries and regions. We need to understand that this history is very closely interlinked with the history of Western colonialism, starting with the Atlantic slave trade from the early sixteenth century onward.

| A VAST AND WEALTHY COUNTRY

Geography teaches us that the DRC, formerly known as Zaire, is an immense country located at the heart of Africa. In the late nineteenth century, the DRC was colonized by Belgium. It became independent on June 30, 1960. The country covers 2,345,409 square kilometers, making it the second-largest country in Africa, after Algeria. The DRC is almost four times the size of France, and shares its 9,165-kilometer border with nine other countries. Although there are no reliable statistics due to the lack of a census, according to current estimates there are around eighty million people living in the DRC, giving it a population density of forty inhabitants per square kilometer. Sixty percent of the country's population are young people under the age of twenty-five, which constitutes a promising human resource for the development of the country.

In addition to the four main languages—Lingala, Tshiluba, Kikongo, and Swahili—more than four hundred dialects are used in the DRC. This linguistic diversity is the pride of the entire population, and could have brought development and self-confidence to the people of the DRC had the colonial language—which, more or less coincidentally, is French—not been introduced. The colonial administration spoke French, so it became the official language, although to this day only a small percentage of the population speak it well; the prerequisite for doing so is school attendance.

As far as the practice of religion is concerned, it must first be made clear that the DRC is a secular state; there is no state religion. Christians constitute the largest faith group, organized into the Catholic, Protestant, and Evangelical churches. Islam, which used to predominate in Kinshasa and the country's eastern regions, is currently regaining popularity. As well as these religions, which came to the country from abroad, particular mention must be made of Kimbanguism, adherents of which worship its founder, Simon Kimbangu, and believe he was sent from God many years ago to liberate the people from the colonizers. Kimbangu, who lived from 1887 to 1951, urged the Congolese to emancipate themselves from colonial rule. In 1921, Kimbangu was arrested because of his subversive teachings, and was held in Katanga, two thousand kilometers from his base and stronghold, until his death in 1951. His followers were persecuted, abducted, and murdered by the colonial rulers. Those who wanted to escape repression by the colonial administration joined other churches, where the ideas of the prophet Kimbangu continued to be preached in secret.

While Kimbanguism played a substantial role in the decolonization of the DRC, it must be mentioned that the Catholic Church was also an important factor in the resistance to General Mobutu's decades-long dictatorship. Cardinal Malula began this fight in the 1980s when he publicly criticized the Mobutu regime's poor leadership, and the resistance intensified in the 1990s, when Mobutu was first compelled to open up the political arena.

The DRC possesses an immense wealth of natural resources and mineral deposits. When you consider the vast size of the country, its position is quite extraordinary: its earth contains gold, diamonds, copper, cobalt, zinc, silver, cadmium, germanium, carbon, manganese, tin, tin oxide, beryl, tantalum, coltan, tungsten, monazite, uranium, nickel, oil shale, bauxite, lead, emeralds, hematite, malachite, phosphates, coal, methane gas, natural gas, and oil.

In addition to its mineral and fossil riches, the DRC is covered in vast swaths of forest. Its total forested area measures an estimated 135 million hectares—6 percent of all the forest in the world, and 47 percent of all the forest on the African continent. Furthermore, parts of the DRC also have huge potential for agricultural cultivation and the farming of livestock. Already the network of rivers that crisscross the DRC generates 98 percent of the country's electricity.

Yet despite this huge potential, the majority of Congolese live in extreme poverty. The DRC is one of the ten poorest countries in the world. There is a striking degree of inequality. Around 80 percent of the population live below the poverty line of $2 a day. Life expectancy is barely fifty-four years.

| HISTORY OF THE DRC

I cannot give a complete account here of the recent history of the DRC, but I must at least make brief mention of the two most important periods.

This large, rich African country was officially ceded to King Leopold II of Belgium at the Berlin Conference of 1885. The Congo Free State became his private property. The king pretended to the outside world that his motives in the country were humanistic, emancipatory, and civilizatory. In reality, he presided over the creation of a cynical and inhumane system unlike any the world had ever seen. Leopold's rule was characterized by the subjugation and abduction of the indigenous population. There was also a system of forced labor: women and children were held hostage in order to compel the men to harvest rubber. Entire villages were wiped out. Anyone who resisted was tortured, or mutilated by having their hands chopped off. Several million people died violent deaths under this system.

This was the price the Congolese people were forced to pay for King Leopold's supposedly humanitarian and civilizing activities.

It wasn't until 1908 that criticism of the crimes for which the king was responsible actually had an effect. The Belgian parliament annexed the Congo Free State, renaming it the colony of Belgian Congo. However, despite this change, the system for exploiting the local population remained in place.

The country didn't gain its national sovereignty until June 30, 1960. This was the result of a long struggle by the Congolese people, led by Patrice Émery Lumumba. The day the Congo became independent, Lumumba spoke the following words: "All of you, my friends, who have fought tirelessly at our side, I ask you to mark this June 30, 1960, as an illustrious date that you will keep indelibly engraved in your hearts, a date whose meaning you will proudly teach your children, so that they in turn might relate to their children and grandchildren the glorious history of our struggle for freedom." The first free elections in the history of the new Republic of the Congo resulted in Joseph Kasavubu becoming the president and Patrice Émery Lumumba the prime minister. However, just a few months after independence, Moïse Tshombe declared the independence of Katanga.

This province was particularly important to the Congo, because the exploitation of its mineral resources accounted for 70 percent of the foreign currency entering the country. The presence of the mines, and therefore also of large Western capitalist firms, largely explains Katanga's political orientation. A few days later it was South Kasaï's turn to secede, under the leadership of Mulopwe Kalonji Ditunga. The two new self-proclaimed heads of state were clearly supported by the former colonial power. After appealing to the United Nations, which sent peacekeepers but held back from intervening against the secessionists, Lumumba turned to the U.S.S.R., and from then on his fate was sealed. Dwight Eisenhower, the U.S. president, was not willing to allow a bastion of communism to be established in the heart of Africa. On January 18, 1961, Lumumba was assassinated, with the complicity of the Belgians and the American secret services.

Following this murder, the crisis in the country continued; finally, amid the ongoing political confusion, General Mobutu seized power in a military coup on November 24, 1965. Mobutu was able to rely on strong support from the United States, which had a considerable interest in maintaining the supply of materials for its industry, and in preventing the Soviet Union from increasing its sphere of influence on the African continent.

For his part, Mobutu's justification for the coup was that it was necessary in order to put an end to the chaos in the country and deliver the riches of the Congo—renamed Zaire in 1971—to its people. In fact, what he did was establish a bloody dictatorship that the Congolese people will never forget, to which corruption, misappropriation of public funds, and human rights violations were endemic. Anyone who resisted Mobutu risked being persecuted, imprisoned, banished, or even murdered. All political parties were banned, and one-party rule was institutionalized in 1973, when the so-called Popular Movement of the Revolution (MPR) was declared the party of state.

Nonetheless, in 1980, a group of thirteen parliamentarians decided to speak out in opposition to their country's undemocratic leadership. They wrote a fifty-two-page letter, addressed to Mobutu, harshly criticizing his administration of the previous fifteen years; then, on February 15, 1982, ignoring attempts to intimidate them, they founded an opposition party called the Union for Democracy and Social Progress (UDPS). Their mission would not prove an easy one: their leaders would be threatened, imprisoned, subjected to physical and psychological torture, or exiled to their native regions.

Political pressure on Mobutu increased, both at home and abroad, and on April 24, 1990, he was forced to introduce a multiparty system. This process resulted in the holding of a national conference* in 1991, bringing together around 2,800 delegates from all sectors of society—representatives of civil society and of the various religions and parties, as well as other holders of public office.

The aim of the conference was to reexamine the history of the Congo and to reconcile the Congolese people with themselves. The past was to be subjected to critical analysis, and transparent, democratic structures were to be created, all in the hope that the community of this nascent third republic could be shaped according to these principles.

---

*The Sovereign National Conference (Conférence Nationale Souveraine, or CNS) played an important role in the incipient democratization of the early 1990s. Laurent Monsengwo Pasinya, then Archbishop of Kisangani, now Archbishop of Kinshasa, was elected president of the CNS. When Mobutu dissolved the CNS in January 1992, large sections of the population protested.

The decisions made at the conference included the determination that a prime minister would be elected to lead the country during a two-year transition phase to democracy. In August 1992, the National Assembly elected the UDPS's Étienne Tshisekedi to this position with more than 70 percent of the vote. The National Assembly chose Tshisekedi because of his moral integrity, as well as his opposition to Mobutu's regime. He had held several positions of high office between 1961 and 1979, but had distanced himself from Mobutu when the latter introduced the one-party system and began to employ increasingly nontransparent methods of government. Tshisekedi then moved to the opposition, and, as the leading figure among the aforementioned thirteen parliamentarians, he seized the initiative to found the UDPS.

Tshisekedi's election as prime minister was greeted with enthusiasm by much of the population. Among Mobutists, however, it provoked fury. Mobutu was used to ruling the country like his own private company. He did not allow the newly elected prime minister a free hand. However, Tshisekedi had already become a tenacious opposition leader who wanted radical changes to the way the country was run.

Mobutu responded by organizing the "ethnic cleansing" of the Kasaï ethnic group—to which his rival belonged—in the province of Katanga, where he was abetted by the provincial governor, Gabriel Kyungu wa Kumwanza. Men, women, and children were killed and expelled as part of this "ethnic cleansing." Those who escaped took refuge in Kasaï Province. Many of their houses and possessions were appropriated by residents of Katanga; tens of thousands of people died.

————

The power struggle between Mobutu and Tshisekedi showed no sign of ending, with Mobutu trying to gain control of the army and public finances. Just three months after he was elected prime minister, Tshisekedi was removed from office. The crisis the country had thought it had survived was only just beginning.

With a view to reinstating the political order introduced by the National Assembly, several rounds of negotiations were scheduled—but in vain. The crisis continued until 1996, when a rebellion started brewing in the east of the country. It was led by Laurent-Désiré Kabila, a former follower of Lumumba who had been involved in repeated uprisings against Mobutu in the east since 1964 and who led a movement called the Alliance of Democratic Forces for the Liberation of Congo (AFDL). Initially, it was said to be just a resistance movement—self-defense on the part of the Banyamulenge. These were ethnic Tutsis who had migrated from Rwanda many years earlier. More recently, they had fled to the mountainous province of Kivu, in eastern Congo, to escape the genocide committed by Hutu militias in Rwanda between April and June 1994, in which more than eight hundred thousand Tutsis were killed. Rwandan Tutsi rebels eventually succeeded in toppling the Hutu government and installing their own leader, Paul Kagame, as the new president of Rwanda. Consequently, from 1994 onward, many Hutus fled Rwanda for the Congo (at the time still known as Zaire), and the Banyamulenge now felt threatened. The arrival of these huge numbers of Hutu refugees was completely uncontrolled. Heavily armed and well-financed Hutu militias, some of which had been involved in the Rwandan genocide, were able to penetrate the Congo. Both the United Nations and certain European countries, including France, supported the trend, and did not even attempt to disarm the militias. The international community also exerted considerable pressure on the Congolese leadership, forcing it to agree to the strategy.

This grave mistake must be seen as a significant cause of the deaths of millions of Congolese men and women. The policy was responsible for exporting the Rwandan conflict between Hutus and Tutsis onto Congolese soil. Hutu militias utilized the Hutu refugee camps in the DRC as rear bases from which, first of all, to pursue the war against the new government in Rwanda, and, second, to attack the Banyamulenge, or Congolese Tutsi.

Paul Kagame, the Tutsi president of the new government of Rwanda, felt extremely threatened by the activities of the Hutu militias, and took the side of the Congolese Tutsi—particularly when they were being targeted and massacred. Defenseless men, women, and children were murdered; many were forced to flee eastward, toward Rwanda. While all this was happening, the Congolese central government didn't say a word. Mobutu had had a good relationship with Juvénal Habyarimana, the Hutu president of Rwanda whose murder had ignited the genocide. In remaining silent, Mobutu made himself an accessory.

While researching this book, I spoke to a friend of mine who is Banyamulenge. He told me: "Our children and grandchildren lived here in Congo. I grew up in Congo, even though I speak Kinyarwanda and still feel connected to Rwandan culture. So I see myself as Congolese. But when the Hutu drove us out and massacred us, I was outraged by the indifference of the Congolese government in Kinshasa."

The flight of the Banyamulenge to Rwanda came in 1996, at just the right moment for Kagame. He set about banding the refugees together, arming them, and sending them back to the Congo to initiate a campaign of conquest. In the words of my friend: "When we arrived in Rwanda we were warmly received by Paul Kagame. He said to us: 'You are Congolese—but does a Congolese man kill his own countrymen? The Hutus have killed your brothers and sisters, your parents and your friends, because they see you as foreigners. Your task now is to avenge the deaths of your people.' Kagame provided us with military training and weapons in no time, and afterward he said: 'Now the moment has come. Attack the Congo. I promise you this mission will be victorious, because the United States and Great Britain are behind me.'"

However, the task Paul Kagame was entrusting to the Banyamulenge was by no means just that of taking revenge. Rather, Kagame was using this motivation to conceal his strategic and economic plan, which was to hound Mobutu out of office and install a leader he trusted in Kinshasa—someone who would help him both to rid himself of the Hutu threat, and to annex the wider region of Kivu, giving him access to its mineral resources.

Meanwhile, the Banyamulenge, now armed and supported by the Rwandan army, grew ever stronger and harder to control and increasingly problematic for the Congolese government. Finally, in 1996, the deputy governor of Bukavu, on the Rwandan border, fanned the flames by deciding that all Banyamulenge should be forcibly returned to Rwanda. This triggered the First Congo War. Congolese government troops fought the Rwandan Patriotic Front, which claimed to be championing the cause of the Banyamulenge. In short: it became clear that the Congolese Banyamulenge had joined forces with other players to form a broad alliance.

Then, on October 23, 1996, Laurent-Désiré Kabila established the aforementioned AFDL. Essentially consisting of five rebel movements and political parties, it was purely an alliance of convenience. Its official aim was to hound Mobutu out of office and restore democracy to the Congo. The Congolese people were enthusiastic about this goal. After thirty-two years of Mobutu's rule, they had had enough. His army was already debilitated; there was resentment toward the dictatorship among the ranks, and Mobutu himself had been weakened by the opposition. All these factors contributed to the ease with which the AFDL was able to advance from Lemera in Kivu to Kinshasa. Its troops crossed the whole vast country in just seven months, despite the terrible condition of the road and communication networks.

However, the declared aim of toppling Mobutu concealed other goals. The AFDL's intention was to split off part of the Congo from the body politic in order to protect and extend the territories of the AFDL's confederate states, Uganda, Rwanda, and Burundi. This is even recorded in article 4 of the AFDL's founding declaration, known as the Lemera Declaration: "Since the Alliance is committed to pan-Africanism, it advocates that an area of 300 kilometers from the Congolese border into the interior be transferred to the neighboring countries Uganda, Rwanda, and Burundi, to protect them from the rebellions that threaten them." This, of course, has little to do with the original idea of pan-Africanism.

AFDL troops took one city after another, finally forcing Mobutu into exile in Morocco on May 16, 1997. The following day, the army of Laurent-Désiré Kabila reached Kinshasa. Kabila himself was in the provincial capital, Lubumbashi, where he declared himself president of the republic and Mobutu's successor. The war that brought about this outcome, supposedly a "war of liberation," cost the lives of several hundred thousand Congolese civilians, as well as those of Rwandan Hutus who had fled to the Congo.

On May 22, Kabila formed his first government. All the opposition forces in the Congo, including the UDPS, were excluded, prompting demonstrations in almost every major city in the country. The movement to oppose Kabila's power had begun.

Kabila acted much as Mobutu had done in 1965: he justified his rebellion and the overthrow of the government by declaring it necessary to put an end to the previous regime. Once he attained power, however, he employed the very same methods he had criticized so vehemently in the past. Public freedoms were suppressed, as were the political activities of all parties except the AFDL. Corruption resurfaced, as did other forms of maladministration that Kabila had deplored during his time in the opposition.

Then, a year after the change of government, a rift opened up between Kabila and his Ugandan and Rwandan allies. "Foreign" officials, who until then had occupied important positions in the government and army, were dismissed and sent back to their home countries. It became apparent that Kabila no longer wished to abide by article 4 of the Lemera Declaration. So Kabila's former allies gathered in the eastern city of Goma and carried out an armed raid on government troops at the Kitona military base. Again, the country was torn apart, and a series of rebel groups formed. The most important of these were the Rally for Congolese Democracy (RCD), supported by Rwanda, which was to occupy a large swath of eastern DRC; the Movement for the Liberation of the Congo (MLC), led by Jean-Pierre Bemba, which occupied Équateur Province; and the militia of the RCD-N, a splinter group of the RCD, led by Roger Lumbala. There were also the militias of the Mai-Mai and other rebel groups. The complex situation resulted in the Second Congo War.

This conflict was primarily about access to the country's mineral deposits, which were claimed by both Uganda and Rwanda. We are still suffering the consequences of this war today: the massacres of the people, the rapes of women and children.

Peace negotiations finally took place in July 1999 in the Zambian capital, Lusaka. The Kinshasa government was supported by Angola and Zimbabwe, the rebel groups by Rwanda, Uganda, and Burundi. Negotiations were conducted under the aegis of the international community, and initially led to a ceasefire. The warring parties also declared their willingness to organize a national dialogue from which no one would be excluded. It was hoped that in this way a new political order could be established. Ultimately, however, Laurent-Désiré Kabila refused to implement the agreed-upon changes, and the war continued.

On January 16, 2001, Laurent-Désiré Kabila was murdered in his palace in Kinshasa, and his son Joseph Kabila* assumed power. This development prompted Étienne Tshisekedi, the leader of the opposition UDPS, to embark on a long tour of America, Europe, and Africa to persuade the international community and friends of the DRC to exert pressure on the government in Kinshasa. The issues at stake were the convening of the previously proposed Inter-Congolese Dialogue, which was held in Addis Ababa in October 2001; the establishment of a new political order; and ending the war, which had completely torn the country apart.

*Right from the start, rumors that Joseph Kabila was not Laurent-Désiré Kabila's biological son played an important role in Congolese society. These rumors are still very politically explosive in the DRC.

On February 25, 2002, the Inter-Congolese Dialogue was resumed in Sun City in South Africa. Again, the parties to the conflict were convened; again, the talks were chaired by the international community; again, the issues at stake were ending the war and appointing new people within the political institutions. The conference was led by Ketumile Masire, the former president of Botswana. This time, in addition to the political blocs involved in the war, representatives of civil society and other political parties were present at the meetings.

On March 14, 2002, the Kinshasa government suspended its participation in the Dialogue on the pretext that the RCD rebel group had carried out attacks on Congolese territory. The Congolese people were appalled by the government's move and staged protest rallies in Kinshasa and Mbuji-Mayi. The international community pressured the Kinshasa government, and managed to get its representatives to return to the negotiating table and continue the Dialogue. Finally, on April 17, 2002, a treaty was reached between the Kinshasa government and Jean-Pierre Bemba, the leader of the MLC. This treaty, signed on the sidelines of the official negotiations at the Hôtel Cascades in Sun City, stated that Joseph Kabila would stay on as president, while Bemba was to be named prime minister.

The treaty was sanctioned by the European Union, but did not gain much approval elsewhere. The RCD and the major opposition parties, including the UDPS, spoke out against it. There was also considerable discontent among the people of the DRC, who saw the treaty as a swindle. The general assumption was that it would lead to further intensification of the armed conflict. Rallies and protest actions followed.

The Kinshasa government and MLC delegations left South Africa, but the opposition parties and the RCD remained in

Sun City and tried to persuade the treaty signatories to return to the negotiating table. They remained intransigent, however, so the UDPS and the RCD decided to form an Alliance for the Protection of the Inter-Congolese Dialogue (ASD). Rather than an ideological alliance, the ASD was purely strategic: it aimed to bring about the continuation of the Dialogue in order to achieve a new, consensual political order. In this, the Alliance was guided by the resolutions and fundamental ideas of the 1999 summit in Lusaka.

The pressure the ASD was able to exert should not be underestimated. After all, the UDPS and the RCD were not political lightweights. The first was one of the biggest opposition parties; it had a presence throughout the DRC and enjoyed the trust of a large part of the population. The second was the largest armed movement and, at that point in time, it occupied almost a quarter of the national territory.

A few months later they were successful. Under pressure from both the ASD and the Congolese people, the signatories to the "Cascades Treaty" returned to negotiate. The Inter-Congolese Dialogue resumed in Pretoria in October 2002 under the leadership of the Senegalese politician Moustapha Niasse.

After lengthy discussions, and after the international community had ramped up the pressure once more, the parties finally achieved a result on December 16, 2002—one that, however, appeared to reward the hostile parties with a war premium. Joseph Kabila would remain in office as president for a transitional period, while four vice presidents, recruited exclusively from the ranks of the armed militias, would be appointed to serve alongside him. Members of civil society and political parties not backed up by armed militias were not included in the government. The contract stipulated a transition period of two years, which could be extended once, after which elections would take place across the DRC. On April 2 and 3, 2003, the agreement was finally sealed, and the Inter-Congolese Dialogue came to an end.

In June 2006, pressure from the international community finally brought about elections. Joseph Kabila emerged victorious, but only thanks to widespread electoral fraud and irregularities. Clashes between government troops and those of Jean-Pierre Bemba inevitably ensued. People were killed and injured in fighting in Kinshasa. Peace was only restored when Bemba was taken prisoner and indicted by the International Criminal Court in The Hague. Strangely, he was not indicted for the crimes against humanity he had committed in the DRC, but for the crimes his troops had committed while fighting alongside Ange-Félix Patassé in the Central African Republic to put down François Bozizé's rebellion.

Kabila, then, remained in power in the DRC. The next five years of his government were marked by a resurgence of fighting in the eastern province of Kivu. At the same time, extensive crimes against humanity were taking place all over the country, as were the arbitrary arrest and murder of politicians and human rights activists. In June 2010, the renowned and highly respected human rights activist Floribert Chebaya, the head of the organization Voix des Sans-Voix—Voice of the Voiceless—was murdered. I had met this passionate human rights defender; the last time we saw each other was in June 2006, at a counter-summit held by the Organisation Manifeste Euro-Africain in Rabat, Morocco.

He and I had a long conversation at a reception arranged for him by a Congolese friend. Around midnight, we accompanied him back to his hotel. On the way there, he advised me to stay in Morocco and not return to the DRC, as the situation there was still tense. In June 2010, I heard via the Manifeste Euro-Africain mailing list that he had been killed. What a terrible thing! I immediately called a friend in Mbuji-Mayi, another human rights activist. He confirmed, through sobs, that Chebaya had been found murdered.

When presidential elections were held again in 2011, all the national and international observers assumed after the count that Étienne Tshisekedi had won. However, by committing massive electoral fraud once again, with the help of the military, Joseph Kabila managed to cling to power.

And so the crisis in my country continued until 2018, just before the elections that enabled us to put an end to this oppressive regime. However, the crisis and the war it engendered have left a country torn to pieces and ready to implode. More than six million people died; women were raped, and rape was used as a weapon of war. Children were exploited in the mines, the population massacred and forced to leave their territory, which was swiftly occupied by people from foreign countries like Rwanda and Uganda. This situation is recurring yet again in Beni, in the northeast of the country, where the war continues to this day. There is also the problem of the influential bigwigs of the former regime, who still occupy the majority of posts in various institutions, in the army, and in the security services.

2

MY LIFE BEFORE EXILE

| MY STUDENT YEARS

The rise in poverty among Congolese people meant many children were unable to go to school. I was lucky: my family had enough money to enable me to attend, and the upbringing and education of their children was always my parents' chief concern. My father, a farmer and cattle breeder, placed great value on education, and spent a large part of his income on our schooling. He always said, "I don't want to have to listen to you later on saying you've failed in life because your father didn't give you enough money to study. If you really do end up achieving nothing, you should say: 'We didn't achieve anything because we didn't take advantage of the opportunity our father gave us to study.'"

By contrast, many of my friends were denied the opportunity to go to school because their families didn't have the financial means. Others attended schools in incredibly dilapidated buildings. The infrastructure and educational support for the majority of schools in the DRC still do not meet the necessary standards. These so-called schools often consist of no more than four walls: the majority have no doors, windows, libraries, or laboratories, and are in terrible condition. All too often, the pupils are motivated but the teacher, lacking proper training and materials, is not. Teachers are also paid low salaries, often several months in arrears. For similar reasons, the administrative machinery doesn't work properly and the officials in charge are not interested in what the teaching staff actually do.

As the public authorities are incapable of fulfilling their responsibilities and ensuring that everyone receives a decent education, children from poor families stay at home. Some parents, out of concern for their children's futures, agree to top up teachers' salaries, and spend part of their income maintaining the teaching in schools. Contributions from parents, many of whom are extremely poor themselves, are nothing like enough to ensure that teachers receive a decent income. This is a problem not only in elementary schools, but in secondary schools and universities as well.

It was in this context that I spent my school days. I learned to value my parents' love, and made a big effort to study even harder and learn even more—not just to keep from disappointing them, but also, and above all, because I already knew back then that I wanted to assume political responsibility later in life, and, in doing so, contribute to the development of my region.

I was highly motivated, and graduated successfully from elementary school. After this, with the support of my older brother, Patrick, I was able to move to another town and continue my schooling there. Patrick had followed our parents' advice and pursued his studies. He had already graduated, and was running his own bookstore in Kananga, as well as another bookstore and a hotel in Mbuji-Mayi.

So it was that in 1987, at the age of fourteen, I arrived in the city of Kananga in Kasaï-Occidental Province, which was where my brother worked. He enrolled me at the Athénée Royal de Kananga school, where I completed the two-year "orientation cycle," the transition phase between elementary and high school. After this, I switched to the Collège Saint Pie X, a Catholic high school with a good reputation. My brother wanted me to have a Catholic education. At this school, I opted to specialize in business and administration.

Right from the first year of my academic training, my brother involved me in the day-to-day running of his business. I would help out with the sales side of things during school holidays, and sometimes also with the bookkeeping.

In 1991, Patrick and I were the victims of a military raid—our store was looted by soldiers. It was no coincidence that we were the targets of this act of vandalism: my brother stocked oppositional political newspapers as part of his range of books and magazines. The papers were displayed in a big glass case in front of the porch. Many people came each day to read about the latest events and discuss political issues. This was at the time when Mobutu had slightly relaxed political restrictions—but the repression wasn't over. The Mobutists had been keeping an eye on my brother's shop, and they did not hesitate to lay waste to his business. It was a terrible day for us. In a matter of hours, Mobutu's soldiers destroyed the fruits of ten years' labor.

When this happened, I was in the fifth year of my studies for my high school diploma. I had one more year to go. What was I to do? Drop out of school and go back to Mbuji-Mayi, or stay in Kananga?

Despite our difficult circumstances, Patrick said, "Emmanuel, don't lose heart. Stay here and finish your studies. The soldiers can steal from our shop, but they can't steal from our minds. I'll keep on making sure you're able to finish your studies." And so, while Patrick moved back to Mbuji-Mayi to manage his businesses there, I stayed on in Kananga for another year. In 1992 I passed my baccalaureate and graduated from school. I returned proudly to Mbuji-Mayi, and with my high school diploma I was soon able to start studying at the university there.

The University of Mbuji-Mayi had been founded only two years before I returned from Kananga. I was glad to have the opportunity to study there. My brother had originally had other plans for me: I was supposed to go and study abroad. He had already started making the necessary arrangements when the shop was ransacked, thwarting his plans.

For me, then, the foundation of the university was a stroke of luck. A number of important people from Kasaï-Oriental, many of whom had been forced to move to Katanga, Kisangani, or Kinshasa to access higher education, had campaigned for a university in the province. It should be mentioned that a great many of the university professors teaching in the DRC today are from Kasaï-Oriental Province. Many Congolese professors who have been offered chairs at foreign universities are also originally from there. Back then, scholarships were still available, thanks to which many of them were able to continue their careers abroad.

Among the best-known Congolese professors from Kasaï-Oriental Province are Kabeya Tshikuku, Raphäel Kalengayi Mbowa, and Georges Nzongola-Ntalaja. But how can it be explained that such an unusually large number of university staff in the DRC are from this remote and long-neglected region? The question is difficult to answer, as there is no obvious explanation—but the phenomenon was instrumentalized by the colonizers to incite people from other provinces against the Kasaï. Specifically, the colonizers portrayed the Kasaï as intelligent, resourceful, and cunning, and implied that they wanted to oppress other Congolese. This strategy cost the Kasaï dearly; it was the impetus for the "ethnic cleansing" they suffered in the provinces of Katanga and Kasaï-Occidental in 1961 and 1962. Mobutu also deployed this colonial logic to oppress the Kasaï and the people of Katanga when Étienne Tshisekedi was prime minister and head of the National Conference from 1991 to 1992.

But back to the foundation of the university in Mbuji-Mayi, the first university in Kasaï-Oriental Province. The reason it took so long for this to happen is that the region was never able to profit from its riches. All the proceeds from diamond extraction and the mining of other ores either went solely to a minority of super-rich people in power, or else were used to build and beautify European cities.

However, the University of Mbuji-Mayi was also founded amid the buildup to the ethnic cleansing of the Kasaï from Katanga in the early 1990s, the historical tragedy to which I referred in the previous chapter. The mining company with concessions in the province was eventually persuaded to make a financial contribution toward the building of the university. Important local businessmen, including Tatu Nkolongo, the owner of the Hotel Tanko, Patrick wa Kanyana, the owner of the Vatican Hotel, and Bukasa Nkumbikumbi, also provided funding; they sponsored the furnishing of some of the offices for the professors, who came to the university from Kinshasa and Lubumbashi once construction was complete. Without the material support these people provided for the university, I would not be writing this book today. I would therefore like to take this opportunity to express my gratitude to them.

In 1993, I enrolled for the preparatory semester in economics. The university's founders had emphasized that preparatory courses must be offered in order to bridge the educational gap that was generally in evidence because of the poor standard of Congolese secondary schools. The aim was to increase the students' knowledge so they would all be sufficiently qualified and able to cope with the work at university.

However, although the university enjoyed the support of the above-mentioned individuals and the standard of teaching was good, it still operated as a training ground for an elite student body rather than as an institution for the education of the masses. When it opened, there were no more than six hundred enrollees across its four faculties. Furthermore, I discovered that many of my fellow students were unable to complete the first year of their studies because they didn't have the money to pay the tuition fees. They lost their accreditation for the courses and were no longer allowed into the lecture theaters. This caused me considerable anguish—after all, there were young people among them who were very intelligent and, above all, highly motivated. They had hoped that by educating themselves they would be able to contribute to the development of the region, and of the country itself. The fact that they would now be excluded fueled our anger, but there was nothing we could do for them: my fellow students and I were bound by the rules of the university.

Lack of education caused by poverty is still a bitter reality in the DRC. I encountered it at primary school, then again in

Kananga—which should be a rich city, with its open-cast mining and diamond reserves. In Mbuji-Mayi, too, young people were being robbed of their education, and thus also of their future.

The education sector is not the only one in the DRC to be affected by poverty and wretchedness. Their impact is felt in every sphere of life and society.

In view of the country's riches, it is simply incomprehensible that its people should have to live in such poverty. This scandalous state of affairs is particularly egregious in Mbuji-Mayi, which is known as the capital of international diamond production.

| MY POLITICAL ACTIVITY

Given this situation, it must be stated that, without a doubt, there is clearly something wrong with the way the country is run. All the successive governments prior to the 2018 elections ran the country badly, creating a whole catalog of problems. One of the principal evils was corruption, which became more or less universal.

The smell of easy money spread everywhere, accompanied by favoritism, tribalism, and the siphoning off of public funds. At the same time, values such as honesty, integrity, and an interest in the common good were actively opposed at every level of the administration. People were not appointed to public sector jobs on the basis of their qualifications; here, too, political clientelism, tribalism, and, often, the boss's favor were what counted. This situation is still ingrained in the mentality of many people in positions of responsibility in the DRC today. Unless there is a shift in the mentality of the population as a whole, it will be hard for the new president to meet its expectations.

I was a student in the first semester of my economics degree at the University of Mbuji-Mayi when I made the firm decision that I would not put up with this any longer. I resolved to step up and take on the historic role that belongs to all young people, and to students in particular: being the ones to bring about change. My decision was made in response to growing injustice and lack of prospects for young people in my country. At the same time, though, it was also based on the experiences of my childhood. Even as a child I had always wanted to fight injustice; I'd been particularly impressed by the fifty-two-page letter of the thirteen parliamentarians who went on to found the UDPS. Now, as a young man, I believed that getting involved in politics was a way for me to contribute, in some small way, toward instigating change in my country.

No wonder my father always commented on how like my grandfather I was. I was told that he, too, had never been able to accept injustice. He had always used the power invested in him by tradition to stand up for two values: justice and sharing. He never ate at home himself, but frequently invited strangers who happened to be passing by his house to come in and eat. It was my grandfather's nature to devote himself to helping others, to the point of self-sacrifice. He loathed injustice—and when the colonizers arrived, this attitude was to cost him his life. They saw him as an agitator, and sent him into exile, far away from his home village. He died in prison a few years later. Even when I was little, my mother was always saying how like my grandfather I was.

So it was that in 1994 I joined the UDPS, the Union for Democracy and Social Progress.

The party was founded in response to the situation in a country both huge and hugely rich, yet the majority of whose people were forced to endure tremendous hardship. The people benefiting from its wealth belonged to an infinitesimally small minority: those in power, who were enriching themselves in the most disgraceful manner. The social model propagated by the UDPS therefore appealed to me. Its top priority was to fight for the establishment of a democratic constitutional state. Like its other supporters, I was convinced that the Congolese people would only be able to choose their political representatives freely and subject them to independent controls in a constitutional state founded on the principles of justice and democracy. We were convinced that the serious and transparent administration of public affairs could then be guaranteed, and the Congolese people would benefit at last from their country's riches.

| MY POLITICAL EDUCATION

My political education began with a course addressing ideological issues. It took the form of political meetings in various districts of the city. This period gave me the chance to accustom myself to my new environment and prepare myself for the world of politics. The courses I attended most frequently were those of Jean-Sans-Peur Mbuyi Mulomba, on the Avenue Maman Yemo next to Bakwa Dianga market. I valued his trenchant analysis of political and social issues, his decisiveness, his political courage, and the hope that this comrade in arms instilled in us. I'd met him before, in 1983, when I was still at primary school. He was our neighbor, but I didn't see him much; he was seldom at home with his family for more than four days in a row. Besides, our

parents had forbidden us to play with his children. I'd heard people say he was from the "second party," but at the time I wasn't
old enough to understand what that meant.

Back then we were still subject to the one-party rule of
Mobutu's Mouvement populaire de la révolution. Every Congolese man and woman automatically became a member of this
party at birth. It was illegal to join any other. Yet the thirteen
parliamentarians who authored the fifty-two-page letter had
dared to found the UDPS. All its supporters were referred to as
"mutu ya deuxième parti"—members of the second party. They
were condemned to live outside the law. These people were ostra-
cized; if their activities were exposed, they, their family, and anyone in contact with them were at risk of arrest, imprisonment,
and sometimes even death.

In Mbuji-Mayi, in 1992, I met Mbuyi Mulomba again—not, this
time, as a member of the political underground, but as an activist freely and openly representing and teaching the politics of the
UDPS outside his house.

I received my political education from him. He talked to us
about the birth and history of the party, and about the aims and
methods of political organization. Mbuyi Mulomba strengthened
our resolve to set fear aside and embark on the pacifist struggle
with the aim of ending Mobutu's grip on power. In his words:

> The UDPS is a party of the masses, founded by thirteen brave
> parliamentarians who said "no" to Mobutu's dictatorship and
> the chaotic leadership of the country. This party is inspired by
> social-democratic values and has the following aims: estab-
> lishing and cultivating a pluralist democracy in order to secure

social progress and good governance; fighting corruption and other abuses; creating a fair and socially minded justice system; securing fundamental human rights and public freedoms; and fighting to ensure that our country remains open to all victims of political intolerance and persecution. On an international level, the UDPS plans to cooperate with all states and organizations that espouse peace, justice, freedom, and progress. The aim of the struggle the UDPS has embarked on is not, however, to free the Congolese people from Mobutu's rule, but to fight imperialism and neocolonialism, as it is only on the basis of these structures that the dictator is able to continue to plunder our country's resources. Our fight will be a long one, but we shall win it. We have decided to employ nonviolent methods, as they are in accordance with the universal principles of the United Nations. If the people are determined, these methods will prove effective.

These were the words spoken by Mbuyi Mulomba outside his house. A whole crowd of people listened to him calmly. Only in the last two years had it been possible to hear such a speech in public.

I was working in my elder brother's bookstore again, in Mbuji-Mayi. I read a lot, especially publications focusing on political issues in our country, and in this way I was able to improve my understanding and sharpen my critical faculties. At the time, though, I was still just an ordinary foot soldier in the party. We were often sent out to distribute leaflets. I was fascinated by politics. I had found a fitting way to contribute to change in our country.

| MY POLITICAL ASSIGNMENTS

AFDL troops arrived in the city in 1997, and with them Laurent-Désiré Kabila. Very soon, though, the whole Congolese population was bitterly disappointed with both the movement and the new president. This was what persuaded me to dedicate myself completely to political life. We were forced to conduct our activities illegally until after Kabila's murder in January 2001.

At this point it should be stated that when he took the city of Mbuji-Mayi, Kabila organized spontaneous elections—conducted not through secret ballots, but by shows of hands—to find replacements for Mobutu's people. The new governor of the province, the new city and district mayors, and all their new officials were elected in this way. The UDPS succeeded in winning these elections because of the party's moral and social integrity, and Jean-Sans-Peur Mbuyi Mulomba became provincial governor.

His period in office did not last long. After six months, he was arrested and taken at gunpoint to Kinshasa, where he was placed under house arrest for refusing to bow to Kabila's burgeoning new dictatorship. Mulomba's arrest was typical of the AFDL's tactics. In the beginning, the party used the UDPS's mobilization of the masses against Mobutu; this made it easier for the AFDL to take Congolese villages and towns on the way to Kinshasa. They instrumentalized the UDPS's ideas to gain power in Kinshasa—but immediately afterward went back to their old ways from the time of the rebellion in eastern DRC. They disregarded the constitutional state, contested the constitution, abused political office to serve their own interests, and muzzled the existing political forces that countered them—including, of course, the UDPS.

It was at this time that I was tasked with setting up a youth organization as part of the local branch of the UDPS. I was to serve as secretary, in my first position of responsibility within the party.

When I was assigned these tasks, all non-AFDL political activity had been banned by Kabila. But I had no idea that I would end up facing oppression and exile. Kabila was not prepared to engage in democratic debate with the country's opposition forces, which could have indicated to him where his ideology was going wrong. We were in no doubt that he would fight all those who refused to submit to his view of the world, and that he would use inhumane and degrading means, including torture. One method, known by its Swahili name, Tumbu Yulu, was to strip the victim naked in a public place, facing the sun, then tie their hands behind their back and whip them. The lashes were aimed at the stomach, and the victim's age determined the number of lashes. All those who opposed Kabila's regime were abused in this way.

The situation in the DRC continued to deteriorate. Secret negotiations took place in 2001: in an effort to resolve the terrible crisis into which the country had been plunged, Étienne Tshisekedi, the UDPS leader, traveled around the world trying to persuade the international community to support the Inter-Congolese Dialogue. At the same time, our local branch of the party was trying to organize—holding conferences and public debates, informing the people about the hoped-for Dialogue, and trying to convince them of the importance of this political step. It was a very difficult period for me. Our mission consumed so much of my time that I had to repeat the final year of my studies. Those of us in the youth wing of the Mbuji-Mayi branch of the UDPS worked incredibly hard, at every possible level. We tried to take on the role of mediator within the party, in an effort to reconcile the different movements that had formed within our branch.

We succeeded in becoming a significant political force in the city. Around this time, I headed a delegation that received Professor Mohamed Hacen Ould Lebatt, the special representative to Ketumile Masire, the facilitator of the Inter-Congolese Dialogue. Masire had been appointed to this role by the United Nations. Lebatt traveled to Mbuji-Mayi to consult with representatives of civil society. He received our delegation in the Motel Nkumbi Kumbi, where he and his delegation were staying.

We presented to him our ideas about the National Dialogue, and reaffirmed our opinion that it should take a similar form to the Sovereign National Conference held during the struggle against Mobutu. In our view, the failure to implement resolutions made at that time was what had brought about the crisis in the DRC. We therefore insisted that an international committee had to be set up, one that was in a position to monitor whether decisions taken were indeed respected and implemented. Professor Lebatt found this a very interesting and attractive idea. He stressed that these questions had not been raised in any other province, and emboldened us in our commitment.

While the Dialogue was in progress, we also kept the city's population informed about developments and raised awareness of the key issues. You could say that we subjected every stage of the talks to careful scrutiny. We set up a group of young UDPS members and student campaigners for change who discussed every

detail of announcements by the different parties and participants, and all the resolutions agreed upon at the various sessions.
We informed the city's population about the conclusions of our
research via the various district branches of the UDPS. And each
time the negotiations stalled, we responded by holding peaceful
demonstrations in the city.

On April 5, 2002, when the Inter-Congolese Dialogue's negotiations failed to make progress yet again, we organized a
conference on the campus of the University of Mbuji-Mayi. The
conference was a sort of "mustering of the troops"—it coincided
with our mobilization in support of Étienne Tshisekedi as candi-
date for the office of interim president of the Republic.

Among those who spoke at this conference was Ngandu Ntumba,
the president of the UDPS's federal committee. He was a princi-
pled and implacable man, strongly inspired by Marxist ideology,
who refused to be intimidated in any way and took a firm stance
against all forms of corruption. He meant a great deal to me. He
died just a few months before the elections in 2011. The circumstances of his death have still not fully been clarified. I spoke to
him on the phone just a few days before he died. "Emmanuel,"
he said, "it's especially important that those of you in exile fight
resolutely now. Here in the DRC, Joseph Kabila has brought
back flogging. They're making arbitrary arrests, too. The people
are being terrorized."

Others who spoke at the conference included Jean-Paul Mbuebue, the federal secretary of the UDPS's youth wing, and Richard
Babadi. I myself spoke at the end of the event, and read out our
declaration concerning the political challenges ahead. This declaration refuted the government's radio and televised assertions

that the Inter-Congolese Dialogue had no significance for the governing officials of the country, and that the office of president of the Republic was not vacant. The declaration I read went on to say that the new political order would require new institutions and new politicians in positions of responsibility, from the president of the Republic right down to local mayors. I also took the opportunity to criticize a succession of Western countries that were pursuing nontransparent schemes to maintain both the dictatorship and the war in the DRC. These schemes would, of course, enable them to continue to exploit the DRC's natural resources unhindered.

Of all the radio and television broadcasters present in the room, only the radio station of the diocese of Mbuji-Mayi was brave enough to broadcast the whole conference and part of the reading of the declaration. Nonetheless, the declaration was a heavy blow to the local powers. They all wanted to know who was backing us.

After the conference, the president of the student committee received an invitation from a representative of the University of Mbuji-Mayi to discuss the possibility of organizing a big joint mobilization against the ruling powers. Meanwhile, Kabila's people were continuing to do all they could to torpedo the Inter-Congolese Dialogue.

We met on a Saturday, established a commission, and started work the following Monday. We spread out among the five university faculties and held mobilization events in all the lectures. I clearly remember the ones at the Pedagogic Institute of Mbuji-Mayi, the biggest pedagogic institution in the province, and at the Department of Commercial Science. My job was to speak at these events. They really were revolutionary moments. My words convinced the students, and motivated them; all courses were canceled so the meetings could take place. The entire Department of Commercial Science attended, and by the time the head of the institute emerged from his office to find out what was going on, it was too late. The spark had caught—our message had gotten across.

The mobilization had gone extremely well, and our campaign had borne fruit. We set the date for the big demonstration: April 17, 2002.

| A DAY OF PROVOCATION AND DANGER

The mobilization campaign we initiated had, of course, also come to the eyes and ears of the security forces and the intelligence service. They were busy doing everything they could to nip our demonstration in the bud—but our motto was that, this time, we would give it our all.

The demonstration was in protest against the fraudulent treaty signed in Sun City between the ruling powers and Jean-Pierre Bemba. We were also supporting the candidacy of Étienne Tshisekedi for the office of interim president. Furthermore, the march was intended to strengthen the role of the unarmed opposition, and thereby also the role of the sovereign people. This, we felt, was especially important; after all, the only reason the warring parties led by Bemba and Kabila were at the center of the negotiations was because they were armed. Every time the rebel groups felt their views were not being taken into consideration, they would withdraw from the talks and carry on fighting. The civilian population, already severely weakened by war, was paying the price. The only ones profiting from the war were multinational companies and the people in power in the DRC.

———

April 17 was a day of great danger. Police and soldiers were positioned along all the main roads of the city from the early hours of the morning. As I left my house to catch the bus to the university, I saw a military truck heading toward the campus. That was when I realized I needed to be properly prepared for the day. I went to a restaurant and ate a large portion of rice and beans; then I went home again to change into clothes better suited to the impending confrontation. Back on the street, I saw that almost all the people on the bus to the university were soldiers. I realized that I could use this opportunity to find out more about the army's strategies. I boarded, sat down beside a soldier and asked him if a military parade was happening today. The soldier said no, that today they had to impose order and calm in Tshikama, the university campus, because the students were planning to take to the streets. I asked him what the reason was for their protest, and whether it had something to do with scholarships, which were unavailable for many years in the Congo; it was the responsibility of the students or the families to pay tuition fees. My "friend," who was more of an enemy, replied: "We don't know anything about it; we just have instructions to maintain order and to use all necessary means to prevent the students from leaving the campus. We're supposed to stop them from marching into town."

He went on, "The students actually know the people in power very well. They know what's going on, and if they're demonstrating, it means something's going seriously wrong. You know, the people in power are only interested in their own and their children's well-being—they don't give a damn about how things are for ordinary people. Even we only matter to them when something's not going well. When the country's calm, they suddenly forget that soldiers also have the right to eat."

I answered him with another question: "But what if the students use force to try to leave the campus—what will you do then?" He replied: "We've been given the order to use all necessary means to prevent them. Our commanding officer will tell us what we have to do."

The bus arrived at the campus, and we got off. Troops were already posted everywhere outside the entrance, but at this point students and academic staff could still go onto the campus without being stopped. I, too, entered the university grounds.

Around nine in the morning we heard a whistle—the signal for us and a group of students to scale the wall around the campus and head to the district's primary and secondary schools. We ordered all the pupils out of the classrooms, and the teachers and principals fled. I particularly remember the moment when we reached the Mulacom school complex. I argued that the first-, second-, and third-grade pupils should be allowed to go home, but one of my comrades challenged me. "Is this how you intend to make revolution, Mbolela?" he said. "If so, you'd better go home and rest. We're fighting for a noble cause; the children all have to join us!"

And so we brought all the children from the surrounding schools to the campus, regardless of their age. At this point, in this chaotic situation, the schoolchildren started to throw stones at the soldiers, who responded by firing into the air. We then tried to leave the campus—despite the fact that it was we who had brought all the pupils into this dangerous situation. I regretted not having spoken out louder against this dubious revolutionary strategy. The soldiers fired into the air again. The more forcefully we pushed in their direction, the more they fired and beat us with their batons. There were a lot of them, equipped with different kinds of firearms and sidearms, and they forced us back onto the campus.

Within thirty minutes of the start of the confrontation, we already had several serious casualties in our ranks. I saw people bleeding; often, they hadn't even realized they were injured. Our main objective was to get off the campus and into the city so we could meet up with our colleagues from the other institutions and march together. Meanwhile, the secretary of the UDPS, Jean-Paul Mbuebue, who had come to the university to bring us news from town and get an overview of our situation, had been arrested.

The military continued to try to blockade us and keep us on the campus, but by now the movement had grown so big that they were effectively no longer in control of the city. Despite the soldiers' efforts, university students managed to thwart the security service's plans by getting off the campus and occupying the big roundabout where UDPS members had already gathered. All public offices were forced to close. Elsewhere, students from the Pedagogical Institute occupied the "de l'Étoile" roundabout, bringing business in Bakwa Dianga market to a halt. The diamond merchants had to shut up shop, along with all the other businesses in the area.

The soldiers were trying to arrest all the students who were still on campus. People started slipping through a hole in the wall that students who couldn't pay tuition usually used on days when there were fee checks. Now people were using the gap to escape the military undetected. I, too, escaped through the gap and joined the others, taking the road that ran past the campus, down toward the district of Tshikama, and from there into the little alleyways that emerged near the courthouse. From there we reached the wide Avenue Kalonji, Mbuji-Mayi's central market, and finally the big roundabout occupied by the UDPS.

The soldiers, now on high alert, followed us in their jeeps. They were armed to the teeth, and some of them pointed their guns at the crowd. Suddenly I saw the bodies of two young men on the ground. They had been hit by bullets. That was the beginning of the end. The next thing I knew, I was lying in a jeep and my shirt was covered in blood. I'd suffered blows to the head and to my left leg, and was bleeding heavily; other comrades were seriously injured. More than 150 demonstrators—men and women, students and UDPS activists—were arrested, taken to the special services' dungeons, and tortured. Some died there, locked up in tiny cells of barely ten square meters. They died from lack of oxygen, or from thirst.

The torments we were forced to endure in the special forces' dungeons cannot be put into words. However, I am convinced that what we went through was part of the struggle to which we had freely committed ourselves. This struggle had already been internalized by millions of Congolese. Arrests could not end it; nor could torture or murder. Patrice Émery Lumumba had begun the struggle. He fought against the colonizers, and paid for his commitment with his life. His legacy was taken up by the thirteen parliamentarians led by Étienne Tshisekedi: they were no longer fighting the colonizers, but their quislings.*

Today, this struggle has become the struggle of all Congolese

---

*Collaborators; after the Norwegian fascist leader Vidkun Quisling (1887–1945).

people, and we have the unshakable belief that one day we will be victorious. I would like to take this opportunity to pay tribute to those who have died in the conflict—including the two young men I have just mentioned. Their only mistake was to demand, by peaceful means, the continuation of the Inter-Congolese Dialogue, and to support Étienne Tshisekedi's candidacy for the presidency of the interim government.

After a week in the special forces' dungeons, we were transferred to the Supreme Court, where a corrupt judge sentenced us to two years' imprisonment in a black site for disrupting the peace and causing public disorder. This disgraceful verdict criminalized the victims while the guilty parties went unpunished. Humiliated and badly injured students were sentenced without any investigation into the incidents whatsoever. The soldiers and police who compiled the records for the court had not even been present when they occurred. This was what they called justice.

In prison, things got even worse for us. The ruling powers, who feared that the UDPS would form an alliance with the RCD, accused us of being a militia. Neither the government nor the police had any scruples; what they were threatening us with was death. It was imperative to find a way to escape, by any means possible. My family made tremendous financial sacrifices to save the life of their son who had campaigned for such an important cause.

They succeeded. I was released—but I was forced to go into exile.

3

ESCAPE FROM THE DRC

I left my country to escape brutality and death. That was in 2002. I had no idea where I would go. I could count on financial support from my family, who sent me money via Western Union, but on the journey I was about to make, there were times when money was of no use whatsoever. In many places it wouldn't even get you a glass of clean water.

I left my country, and felt like a nomad. I went first to Brazzaville, soon moving on to Cameroon, to Nigeria, Benin, Burkina Faso, and finally Mali. I became a hanger-on: I suddenly found myself traveling with group after group of strangers. Some were the same age as me, some older, others younger; there were even children among them. We would join up and travel part of the way together. Where had all these people come from, and why had they set off on their journey? At night, in buses or lorries, we would tell each other our stories. Some of the people I met were fleeing the war in eastern Congo—they told me they'd had to tramp through equatorial forest for days in order to escape the country. Their faces betrayed the extent of their suffering, the painful memories they carried within them. Some had had to watch their parents being burned alive. Others had been raped, or were forced, under threat of death, to rape their own parents, brothers, and sisters. I remember one fellow traveler who told me his mind was still completely back in the DRC. He couldn't forget what he'd experienced. The terrible images of soldiers raping and abducting his sisters refused to leave his head. He kept asking, over and over again, if he would see them again one day.

However, not everyone was fleeing persecution. Others had left home to seek their fortune elsewhere. They said: "Mboka eza ya kokufa, bakonzi na biso baza na mawa na biso te, bazo sala kakan mpona ba famille na bango. Soki otali bien, bana na bango nionso baza kaka na poto." Which means something like: "The DRC is in chaos, and our leaders have no pity for us; the only thing they're interested in is the well-being of their own families. Just look—all their children live in Europe!"

The stories I heard along the way reinforced my conviction that our struggle was both important and appropriate—because security guaranteed by democracy is greater than security established by force of arms.

I encountered no serious problems on the journey from Brazzaville to Mali. Generally speaking, there is freedom of movement; it basically comes down to the contents of your wallet. If you have money, you can easily travel from one country to another. In this sub-Saharan region, crossing borders always means cooperating with border guards.

However, those fleeing political persecution or armed conflict often have no idea where they are heading. These men, women, and children had not been able to prepare for their journey.

Others—the ones who were "searching for life," as they often put it—knew where their path would take them: to Europe. But even the travelers who fell into this category often didn't know where exactly they were going, or which countries they would have to cross. So on this journey you seldom continued in the company of the same people with whom you had entered a given country. You usually traveled on with people you had only just met in that new place—provided, of course, you had the necessary means to do so, or were able quickly to access those means. Those who couldn't plan their journey, who had no relatives in Europe or in their home countries, were left behind. I made friends, only to lose them again each time I left for a new country. Nevertheless, we swapped phone numbers and, most important, e-mail addresses so we could stay in contact.

The farther I traveled, the more I encountered on the road not only my Congolese compatriots, but fellow travelers from other places, too—Central and West African countries, above all. The stories I heard from them were almost the same as those of my countrymen and -women. I also heard tales of social and cultural persecution. This was how I first became aware that women and girls were fleeing the practice of female genital mutilation. One woman I met on the road told me her sister-in-law had insisted that her daughter be circumcised. This had caused a rift between the woman and her husband's family; she had been forced to separate from her husband, take her little daughter, and leave the country. The woman explained to me that, in cases like these, family members were often exacting retribution. Women like her sister-in-law who were unable to bear children as a consequence of circumcision would try to impose the same fate on other women.

Often, too, people cited economic reasons for their migration.

A young Cameroonian, for example, told me he wanted to go to Europe in search of a better life. He said that the president of his country, who had been in power for years, did nothing for the people. The young man was unemployed, and didn't even have enough money to give his parents a decent burial. He talked about a young emigrant who had gone to Europe; in just a few months this man had earned so much money that he was able to support his family, and had even been able to pay for his brothers to go to school.

All these stories showed me that there are those who leave to start a new life, and those who leave to save their lives. The more I heard, the more I regretted that I'd had to leave my country. The battle must be fought within the country itself! I told myself that one day I would go back and bring about change that way, not so much for my own family, but for the country and—why not?—the whole African continent. The chaotic state of the DRC is absolutely comparable with the situation in the majority of other African countries, as I came to realize by listening to all my fellow travelers' stories on my journey into exile.

In Brazzaville I met a lot of other refugees, many of whom had left the DRC during the Mobutu era. There were also members of our political party, the UDPS, who had been forced into exile, as I had. But I didn't like the atmosphere in Brazzaville. The country was at war: its president, Pascal Lissouba, had been ousted by troops led by Denis Sassou-Nguesso, and during my time there the saber-rattling was far from over. Many refugees from the DRC were also being arrested and deported back to Kinshasa, so it would have been very risky for me to stay in that country.

———————

I set off for Cameroon. I had met someone in Brazzaville who told me that his brothers lived in Yaoundé, the capital of Cameroon, that they'd been there for many years, and that you could be safe there. I had no other options, so I followed him.

Once we arrived in Cameroon, though, it all got rather complicated. My traveling companion from Brazzaville couldn't find his brothers, so although we didn't have much money left, we had to stay in a hotel. How long would we be able to afford that?

In Yaoundé I met several other Congolese people who advised me to go to the city of Garoua. The office of the United Nations High Commissioner for Refugees was there, they said, and I would be able to apply for asylum. Never having thought I'd be a refugee, this idea had never occurred to me, and I wondered whether such a plan was actually feasible. It was only after a week that I decided to take the bus to Garoua. Unfortunately, when I arrived, the office of the UNHCR was shut. According to some Congolese and Chadian refugees we met in town, there was indeed an accommodation center for asylum seekers; they had been staying there, but it had closed. It was supposed to re-open, they said, but when? I waited a few weeks, but the office showed no sign of reopening. A new Congolese friend asked if I would accompany him to Benin: the UNHCR office there functioned well, he said.

We made preparations for our departure. In order to get to Benin, though, we had to cross Nigeria—which was tricky, as controls at the Nigerian border were very strict. I had no travel documents with me, and wondered how I should proceed. However, the friend I was traveling with seemed well acquainted with the rules of this route. "Don't worry," he said. "We're still in sub-Saharan Africa, after all."

It was a Saturday when we set off for Nigeria in a jeep. My traveling companion assured me that entering the country was less a matter of whether or not you had papers than of how much money you had in your pockets and whether you knew how to "cooperate." This understanding of cooperation enabled us to enter Nigeria. We reached the city of Bauchi, then went on to Kano, a city where the Christian and Muslim populations are constantly clashing. We had to be extremely cautious, and stayed almost a whole week with a Congolese compatriot. The fact that I was a Christian made our stay especially risky. It was only a week later that we were able to get a ride in a truck going to Benin.

Our understanding that the UNHCR office in Benin was functioning was very much mistaken. In this country, we met refugees who were having to fend entirely for themselves. Some of them told us that the police had even entered their camp and beaten them because they had insisted on their right to be taken to a safe third country. I was not exactly encouraged by this news. Quite the opposite: I was at a loss, and didn't know what to do next. At least I could glean some hope from the fact that I was able to call home and ask my family to send money. Nonetheless, the life I was now being forced to lead was extremely disconcerting. I had never left my homeland before. On top of this, the circumstances of my journey were unusual, and I didn't yet know the rules of the game. The refugees I met here were living in conditions I found frightening. I wondered whether it really was the right decision to seek protection in this country, in these circumstances.

I was condemned to inactivity for two months—so I decided to travel on to Mali. The route took me through Burkina Faso, where I spent only a few days, dealing with some formalities and changing buses.

| MY ARRIVAL IN MALI

In December 2002 I arrived in Bamako, the capital of Mali. I lived with a certain Serge M., who had been commended to me by my friend in Yaoundé. My friend's friend is my friend, as the saying goes. Later on, we did indeed establish a close friendship of our own. Serge had already been living in Mali for more than five years. He had a great many Malian friends, was well-known in various parts of the city, and spoke the local language, Bambara, perfectly. People from pretty much every African country were constantly coming and going at his house. It seemed that every Central African traveler who washed up in Bamako had to pay him a visit. Usually, Serge would receive the travelers, help them find an apartment, and assist them with all the measures they needed to take in order to travel on. Serge was a very hospitable person. Malians respected him, especially those who had been to the DRC.

The people passing through Serge's home came from Cameroon, Guinea, Nigeria; Serge would receive phone calls from Algeria, Morocco, even Europe. Almost without exception, the travelers I met at his house all had the same story to tell: they'd had to leave their homeland because of the desperate situation there, because of war, dictatorship, or political instability. The majority of the refugees were young people who cursed the political leadership of their countries. They couldn't see a future for themselves at home; their only hope was to leave. Serge's house was a crossroads, a center of debate. Sometimes our conversations were interrupted by the ringing of phones: travelers who had headed north confirming their arrival in Algeria, Morocco, or elsewhere. Other callers told us about their ordeals, and informed us of precautions we should take on our own journeys. Sometimes we heard cries of joy; at other times we were given tragic news. This was also how we would hear of the death of a fellow traveler in the desert.

The stories of my temporary housemates at Serge's place made a deep impression on me. I was struck not only by their determination to get away, but also by their overwhelming desire to help their families. I remember one boy who never tired of repeating that he was going to buy his mother a car with the money he would earn in Europe. He wouldn't tell her about his plan, though—he wanted to surprise her by turning up at the port with the car. He was prepared to take on any conceivable form of work in order to achieve this, even if it meant slaving away for twenty hours a day. After that, he said, he wanted to buy a plot of land and build a nice house.

Others had the idea of saving up to buy big buses—the kind you see on TV—which they would then make available for public transport in their homelands. They wanted to do what their countries' politicians—whose responsibility it was—were incapable of doing. In short: everyone was seeking something abroad that they couldn't find at home, and all were driven by the desire to make their families happy.

I stayed in Mali for almost a year. I hoped to return to the DRC and continue the struggle, so I waited for the outcome of the second round of the Inter-Congolese Dialogue before making a decision. I thought the resumption of the Dialogue would lead to the signing of a comprehensive treaty, one that would establish a new political order in the country, based on the values of democracy, justice, and good governance. I hoped the institutions would be led by competent, credible officials who were mindful of the common good. I'd bought myself a little radio, on which I was able to listen to the news that came out of my country day by day. I shared the information I picked up from Radio France International, the BBC, and other broadcasters with my countrymen and -women, and they responded by nicknaming me "President." Most of them took a pessimistic view, and didn't believe there would be a good outcome to the negotiations. They kept telling me, "Président, luka nzela okende, batu wana bakosala eloko ya malonga te"—"President, it's better for us to try to find ways of getting away; the people conducting these negotiations won't achieve anything good." I, on the other hand, was optimistic, and tried to convince them. I was already calculating that, after returning to the DRC, I would use the two-year transition period to democracy that was called for in the talks to finish my studies. After that, I would embark on my political career. I believed that politics was a way for me to contribute to the kind of change that would advance the development of the country.

But it was my countrymen's analysis that would prove correct.

| DISAPPOINTED HOPES

On April 3, 2003, the Inter-Congolese Dialogue concluded in the South African city of Pretoria. A comprehensive agreement was reached, but it effectively rewarded those who had been parties to the conflict. Preference was given to the Kinshasa government, the RCD-Goma, the MLC, and other military groups, while the unarmed opposition—the UDPS in particular—was relegated to the background. It was as if we had been told that we ought to have taken up arms and killed and raped our countrymen and -women, because this was the only way we would be rewarded with ministerial office.

The country's administration during the transition period was regulated in a form that does not exist anywhere else in the world. The infamous "1+4" formula guaranteed that four vice presidents would hold office alongside the president. Each of these vice presidents would lead an autonomous government commission. I realized that the agreement would allow the Mobutists to return to power, while leaving the Kabilists firmly in charge.

The following day I went to an Internet café in the city that was frequented by many Congolese, and read the information on the UDPS website. I came across a press release from the UDPS's representation in the Benelux countries. The communiqué expressed regret that 80 percent of the politicians who had participated in the negotiations and had been appointed to positions of responsibility in the interim government were not conscious of the task that had been assigned to them. It commented that the majority of these politicians were intent on continuing to exploit the country's resources, and emphasized that the UDPS was not prepared to be part of a government that, by acting in this way, increased the people's suffering still further.

When I finished reading the press release, I realized that we had made no progress at all. The country for which Patrice Émery Lumumba had shed his blood was now, once again, being entrusted to the murderers of the Congolese people and exploiters of its resources. Ten years after the national sovereign conference ended in failure in 1992, the scenario was being repeated.

I lay awake all night, thinking. I had to make a decision. I couldn't wait things out here any longer, nor did I want to. There was no future for me in Mali. I couldn't claim asylum here, either. Either I had to go back to my homeland and face the same threats and persecution from which I had fled, or I had to continue my journey, in search of a country that would grant me asylum. That night, I recalled the horrendous treatment to which my friends and I had been subjected. I remembered my comrade Jean-Paul Mbuebue, whom I had had to leave behind in the central prison of Mbuji-Mayi. I also remembered the two young men who had been killed at our demonstration, and the torture Mukeba Dierbé, a boxer who had been arrested by the police after joining our demonstration, had suffered . . . All this I remembered, yet I couldn't find a satisfactory solution for my predicament.

Finally, I made the decision to continue my journey into exile. I wanted to go to a country where I would be able to continue my struggle. I wanted to find a country where my dedication to establishing a state where justice and democracy prevailed would be valued by the important decision makers of this world.

So I would leave—but where would I go? From then on, this question left me no peace. Finally, in my state of uncertainty, I decided to join some people who were preparing to set off for Algeria. My aim was eventually to reach a country where order, peace, and, above all, freedom reigned. Such countries are extremely rare on the African continent, even in North Africa. So I had to get used to the idea of making my way to Europe and applying for asylum there. Some of the people I'd seen depart while I was in Bamako had called us and told us that they were already in Europe.

Heading for Europe, though, meant starting a new phase in my life. I had gone to a Catholic school, and had developed a very rational attitude. It wasn't easy for me to imagine embarking on an adventure like this. I had stuck it out in Bamako in the hope that, from there, I would be able to return to my homeland. I didn't want to set off at random—my journey from Burkina Faso to Mali had already been a dangerous one. I had no papers, so I'd had to remain silent for the entire journey in order not to reveal my Central African dialect and raise suspicions that I might have entered the country illegally. There had been spies along the route, too; they didn't actually stop illegal immigrants from continuing on their journey, but they cooperated with border guards to extort money from travelers. By this point in my travels, if not before, I had understood that the poverty of border guards all over the African continent was responsible for creating this situation.

And so I called my family to inform them of my decision. It took more than a month for me to convince them of my plan. They had many reservations, and were very afraid, as they had seen the pictures on TV of migrants who had drowned in the Mediterranean. My mother, in particular, didn't want me to leave Bamako. I finally gained her approval, but only on the following condition: on no account was I to get into a pirogue—a fishing boat—in order to reach Europe. I had to promise them that I would wait for an opportunity to travel by plane. A few weeks after this conversation, my parents sent me $1,000 via

Western Union. It wasn't going to be easy for me to contact them on the next stage of my journey.

The stretch from Brazzaville to Bamako had been relatively straightforward; it was easy to travel in informal groups of two or three. This would be very far from true of the section that lay ahead. It required detailed preparation. We would be entering a new region, with new inhabitants, new cultures, and new languages. Pretty much everything would be new to us. So far, the border guards had had difficulty identifying our nationality at a glance. From now on, our skin color would betray us from afar. The same was true of our language. Cultural differences also needed to be taken into account. We were quite used to covertly slipping a few banknotes into a border guard's hand so that he would let us through. But did such practices exist in North African countries? Added to all this was the fact that we would be crossing the Sahara.

Fortunately, Serge was very familiar with the details of the route. You might even have thought he had traveled it himself, which wasn't the case. He was constantly in touch with migrants who had set off and then been forced to stay longer than planned at some point along the route because they had no money. Within the system Serge had established, these people became "facilitators." They served as intermediaries, or replaced old intermediaries when they traveled on. Along the entire route, it had to be a certainty that the intermediaries were fully aware of the current situation. At all times they had to be acquainted with the operational mechanisms of the route. Sometimes they even had to know the names of the officers conducting checks on crucial roads on a given day.

It took me two months to prepare for the journey. I gathered all the information I could about the route, and tracked down friends who had come to Bamako with me and had already traveled on. Finally, some other would-be travelers and I found an opportunity to make the journey from Bamako to Gao, a small city in northeastern Mali, right on the edge of the Sahara.

| DEPARTURE FOR GAO

We left for Gao at 6:00 p.m. one evening in September 2003. The bus was completely full; I recognized some people from our "network."

There were no problems at all on the first stretch of the journey. We talked about everything and nothing; there were no police checks, and for two days and nights the bus drove along the cross-country highway. The next morning, just outside Gao, we arrived at the ferry across the Niger River. We had to get out; the bus was ferried across first, and then it was the passengers' turn. We were all supposed to get back on the bus on the other side of the river in order to be taken to the city train station. But this was when we encountered the first difficulty. It seemed that only the merchants who had come to do business would be able to continue their journey without a problem. For us, it would have been reckless to drive on—we could see a police roadblock a little way ahead, where they were checking people's papers. What my traveling companions and I had in our hands were not papers issued by the migration authorities; ours were purely informal documents that would be of no use to us. And so, after crossing the river, we decided to let the bus drive off without us.

We split into groups of four and tried to find our local contact, with whom we were to lodge during our time in Gao. This woman was supposed to make all the necessary arrangements for our onward journey. Apparently, the plan was for us to be taken to Kidal in a 4x4 pickup.

We reached our contact's house after walking for an hour. She had already been informed that we were on our way. The new arrivals were divided into seven groups and put up in various different locations.

Gao is a small town. New arrivals are immediately noticed, and anyone who takes them in is obliged to register this information with the police right away. Although we had made ourselves scarce after being ferried across the Niger, news of our arrival quickly spread through town. That very night, the police were suddenly knocking at our door. Following a discussion with two members of our "network," three young women who were traveling with us were called over. They disappeared, and did not return until the following morning. When they came back, they were very dejected. Their faces said it all. No one had the courage to ask them what had happened. That was when I realized why the women had been split up and distributed among all the subgroups.

All day I felt agitated and helpless because of the violence to which they had been subjected. I realized that the members of our network had done a deal with the police: they would hand over female passengers in exchange for being allowed to go about their business. The importance of our political struggle was brought home to me yet again. If our countries were well governed and concerned about the welfare of their people, these women would not have had to leave home and be forced to endure such degradation. In our current situation, we had to submit to the inhumane rules of the journey. On our third night there, the police came again. We were forced to pay 1,000 CFA francs [$1.69] per person, and the women were abducted once again.

| FROM GAO TO TINZAOUTEN

We left Gao in a pickup truck. The driver preferred to travel at night so as not to attract the attention of the police. For days we drove across the Sahara, only occasionally taking the highway. We passed several military camps. Our driver carried a gun. We drank water stored in tubing, made warm and unpalatable by the heat. In the desert, money loses its value—the only thing that matters is saving your own life. We travelers stopped talking to one another. Sometimes the driver lost his way. When this happened, he would stop and pray to help himself find the track again. The 200-kilometer journey from Gao to Kidal was far more arduous than the 1,400-kilometer journey from Bamako to Gao. When at last we arrived in Kidal, the driver handed us over to another contact person, an elderly man who had lived there for many years, who was supposed to get us to Tinzaouten. He sorted things out for us and managed to find a 4x4 jeep. Each passenger had to pay the old man an "admission fee."

Eventually we were divided up and put on two pickups, each of which had space on their load beds for a maximum of twelve people. There were fifty migrants squeezed onto each one, squashed up against each other like sardines. As always, they made sure that there were women in both groups. We watched and said nothing as the two drivers squabbled over the female passengers—"Hey, you, get in here!"—"No, this one travels with me!"

We set off from Kidal to Tinzaouten. Here, too, the two drivers avoided the highway for fear of being stopped. They only took the main road at certain points, and then only for a short time. We drove in convoy—it was the first vehicle's job to let the second know if it fell into an ambush.

One night we were stopped at a roadblock. We didn't know who had stopped us. We were forced to get out, and a long discussion ensued with the driver, who finally ordered us to pay 3,000 CFA francs [$5.14] per person. We complied with the demand—nonetheless, the female passengers were again separated from the group and taken away. We were made to spend the night there and wait until the women were brought back. This was apparently how it worked here. We were right to assume that, here, too, the driver was complicit in the blackmail; he disappeared that evening and didn't return until morning. No one dared to ask where he had spent the night. Later, one of the female passengers confided in me that the driver and their aggressors had known each other well—they had shared the money, and also control over the women.

We finally arrived in Tinzaouten, in southern Algeria—a no-man's-land in the middle of the Sahara—at around 10:00 p.m. We had only just crossed the border when it suddenly became clear that an Algerian military jeep was following us. Our driver hastily ordered us to get out, and we ran away as fast as we could to hide in the dunes. That day I felt I'd had enough of life. I was at the end of my strength. Fortunately, the soldiers followed the jeep, not us. Although it was very cold, we lay there for more than an hour so we wouldn't be discovered. Then we set off to look for the "ghettos" in the town: "ghetto" was our name for the provisional, rickety dwellings where migrants lived. It took us three hours to find them. Some of the women had stayed where they were, lying in the sand; they didn't have the strength to move. It was only when we reached the ghettos that the "chairmen"* of the different communities instructed their people to equip themselves with canisters of water and go and look for the women.

Once we'd found the ghettos, we had to find a place to sleep. Each community housed its own people, so we went to the Congolese ghetto—but no one here cared in the slightest about their fellows. We were twelve new Congolese arrivals, and many of our countrymen and -women had already been living there for some time. We quarreled over drinking water. More than thirty people were forced to live crammed together in a space of about ten square meters. Men, women, and children all slept on the ground. If you were lucky enough to find a spot, you had to remain in the position you lay down in; you couldn't move. It was only because we were exhausted that we managed to fall asleep. We slept through till the following morning.

| LIFE IN THE GHETTO

When we arrived in Tinzaouten, there were four ghettos: Congolese, Cameroonian, Liberian, and Nigerian. Each community had its own organization; each had its chairman. The chairman was responsible for his countrymen and -women; he always knew who

---

*"Chairman" is the title given to the informal heads of the respective communities, which are organized by country.

was in Tinzaouten and who was traveling on into the Algerian interior. He instructed new arrivals in the rules of the ghetto, the site of which was known as the "territory." The chairman's contacts could get hold of a car, or documents for people without papers, to enable them to travel on to Algeria.

The morning after our arrival, our chairman explained the rules we had to stick to on our "territory." There were rules that all communities were required to respect, and specific ones that depended on your country of origin. Among the rules everyone had to observe was that every new arrival had to pay €20. Anyone who wanted to travel on had to pay another €10. The chairmen used this money to keep the ghettos going, and to ensure they had funds at their disposal in case of emergency. Sometimes a chairman and the members of his "office" were able to finance their own onward travel in this way. Another general rule was that no convoy was allowed to take young Nigerian women with them without first obtaining the consent of the Nigerian chairman. The duty of solidarity among fellow countrymen was enforced by all communities.

By far the most striking thing about these "territories" was the existence of the Nigerian prostitution network. The clients for this sex work were mostly Algerian policemen, who were consequently well disposed toward the Nigerian chairman.

There was often conflict between the different ghettos over claims to leadership. This conflict was frequently instigated by members of the Nigerian community, who, on top of the business they did with travelers, were also involved in drug trafficking and prostitution networks. Because of all their nefarious schemes, they had to enforce greater discipline and control to guarantee the security of their "territory." Dealings with women in the various ghettos turned out to be another source of conflict.

If the chairman of another community saw a woman he liked, he would send out his people to bring her to him by force.

Yet again I witnessed the violence to which women traveling in these regions are subjected. Young women from Nigeria were particularly badly affected. Members of their own community would sexually abuse them and sell them to people from other ghettos for money. It was terrible for them. The money from these transactions went directly to the chairman. In exchange, he would guarantee the "protection" of these women, who were often extremely young. I kept asking myself into whose pockets Nigeria's immense wealth was disappearing. The country has huge reserves of oil, yet apparently it was impossible for these young Nigerian women to be guaranteed protection. They were mercilessly abused, forced to live in degrading conditions, and exposed to a high risk of infection. I was shocked to see under-age girls in the Nigerian ghetto who were pregnant. I remember one of these young women, heavily pregnant, who kept vomiting. In what circumstances would she have to give birth?

In many cases, the young Nigerian women were accompanied by a man who was "responsible" for them. This man had brought the women this far, and they had to follow him everywhere, all the way to Europe. The women were usually completely under his control, forced to obey his every instruction. Some of the people who had been living in the ghetto for some time before my arrival explained that the women were being brought to Europe by their "bosses" to do "business" there. This was not only the fate of women from the Nigerian community; women from all the ghettos were forced into the same or similar conditions. Then there was the violence of the soldiers and police officers who terrorized them and abducted them at night. The difference was that the Nigerian women were usually abused by men from the ghettos, whereas the higher-ranking soldiers preferred women from other African countries. These women would return in the morning with mineral water and food, which led to jealousy and sometimes even fights. The women who went with the policemen enabled the "contact people" to get Algerian visas. Sometimes, though, a policeman would take a shine to a particular woman; when that happened, he would keep her and only let her go two weeks later. Women who went with policemen had a better chance of getting a temporary visa, or a Malian passport that had been confiscated from another migrant by the Malian authorities.

In Tinzaouten I also saw the graves of several men and women who had died in a confrontation between Nigerians and Cameroonians.

In the two weeks we spent in Tinzaouten, we washed only once. We drank water from a well. I was on good terms with the women in the ghettos, and sometimes they gave me mineral water they'd been given by the soldiers. There was very little food available, and we couldn't afford to be fussy. Sand got everywhere, including into the food, as a strong wind was constantly blowing.

At last the chairman found a contact person for us. We would be taken to Tamanrasset, a town in southern Algeria, in two pickups.

| AMBUSHED

The journey to Tamanrasset was the hardest part of my odyssey. We set off on foot, on a Wednesday night, at around 10:00 p.m. The pickup trucks were waiting for us in the desert about a kilometer outside town in order to avoid police checkpoints. A guide, who knew where the vehicles were hidden, went on ahead; before we could drive off, each traveler had to give him €5. We got into the two pickups and the journey commenced. Once again, we traveled in convoy, so that if one vehicle broke down, the other could come to its aid, and to ensure that neither jeep got lost. I wondered, though, how this would actually help us if we did break down—both jeeps were already overloaded, the passengers again squashed together like sardines.

We drove until 2:00 p.m. the following day without encountering any difficulties. We were tormented by hunger and thirst, but we had already gotten used to that. Then, in the afternoon, we broke down. It took over an hour to repair the truck. Fortunately, we were able to continue our journey—but just twenty minutes later, a group of people materialized in front of us. All of them were wearing djellabas* and turbans. They motioned to the drivers to stop, and ordered us to get out and lie on the ground. This wasn't going to be a case of simply paying a toll.

The men searched us thoroughly, one after the other, forcing each traveler to undress, and even examining their anuses. Several women had hidden money in their private parts; the men found a total of $800. Another woman had no money on her; they beat her, and threatened to keep her with them. From me they stole $520 that I had stashed in my trousers. Two women

---

*A long, flowing traditional garment worn in the countries of the Maghreb. Men usually wear plain djellabas, while women's tend to be brightly patterned.

lying beside me had their mobile phones taken. In the space of a quarter of an hour, we were robbed of all our worldly goods.

We picked ourselves up and continued on our way. No one said a word. Men and women were weeping. All of us were wondering whether what we had just been through was a terrible coincidence, or whether the two drivers were colluding with the thieves. I couldn't work out the answer.

The following day, at around 8:00 p.m., our drivers suddenly ordered us to get out. We were still in the middle of the desert, but they told us we had arrived in Tamanrasset. They pointed to an electricity pylon in the distance and told us to head that way to get to the city. Then the drivers vanished; they were afraid of getting caught by the police, who were known to search the area for traffickers.

And so we started walking, without knowing where we were going. After a while the pylon, which had started off ahead of us, suddenly seemed to be at our backs. We tramped on until midnight, but even after four hours we still hadn't managed to reach the pylon. We were all exhausted. People in our group gradually started collapsing from hunger and thirst. It was also very, very cold. No one came to our aid in the desert. The women were crying, but no one paid them any attention. Everyone was just afraid for himself.

For the second time on this journey, I felt that I'd had enough of life. I'd left my country in order to save it—would I now lose it here, in the desert? At home, I had risked my neck for an important cause. I would have gone down in the annals of history; my death would have been mourned by my family, friends, and acquaintances. Here, in this desert, I could see Death on the prowl; we were in danger of being taken by him unawares. Who would inform my parents? In this group of travelers, I was the only one from my part of the world. These thoughts were overwhelming, and I realized that I, too, had begun to sob. My parents had been right to warn me against this. Now it was too late—we were lost, and completely disoriented. The pylon was still visible, yet it seemed impossible for us to reach it. Before we left, the chairman had told us what to do if we got lost in the desert: stay in one place, rest and sleep. Someone in our group reminded us of this advice, but no one listened to him, and we went on marching. After another hour had gone by, I mustered the courage to speak, and again reminded people of the chairman's words. This time it worked, and they listened. We stopped and huddled in the sand to rest.

As dawn was breaking, we heard the sound of an engine—but it was an Algerian police vehicle. We didn't call for help, as we would just have been thrown into prison and sent back to Tinzaouten. Finally we were overcome by exhaustion and fell asleep.

We were lucky. The chairman in Tinzaouten had called our driver, who told him that he'd made us get out in the desert a few kilometers outside Tamanrasset. That chairman then spoke to the chairman in Tamanrasset, who told him we hadn't arrived. So the Tamanrasset chairman sent out a team of five people to look for us. When I saw these five people approaching, I wondered whether they, too, had gotten lost. Miracle of miracles: they had come to save us! We followed them for an hour, and reached the city at last.

And so we arrived in Tamanrasset—but we had lost everything we owned. When we told our new friends about our experience, they said such things happened all the time. What was important was that we had gotten out of it alive. Many people had died in the desert. They added that we were lucky to have been carrying money; otherwise the bandits would certainly have shown no mercy. They might well have killed some of our group.

When I heard this, I stopped worrying about the lost money. I didn't have a single cent left with which to call home, but I thought: Isn't it better, in any case, not to say anything? If I told my family what had happened, they would surely balk at my continuing my journey.

Some of my fellow travelers called people they knew in Europe, but I didn't know anybody there; there was no one I could count on for assistance. Sometimes, though, I saw callers being denied support—when they explained their situation, their friends and acquaintances simply didn't believe them. The only remaining option for most people was to work in the fields, and on construction sites in the city, in order to scrape together the money to travel onward.

| LIFE IN TAMANRASSET

Tamanrasset is the crossroads for all the migrants coming from Niger, Mali, and Libya. I would end up staying there for more than four months.

I met up with some friends I'd met on my travels in Benin. They had taken the route through Niger. And there were others I had gotten to know in Mali, who told me they'd been stuck in Tamanrasset for five months already. I met men, women, and children from my homeland, from Cameroon, from Guinea, Mali, Niger, Côte d'Ivoire, Liberia, Sierra Leone, Nigeria, and other African countries.

Life in Tamanrasset was harder than in the other way stations I had encountered so far. There were no migrant ghettos here. We slept on the street, in the open air; we spent all our days and nights there, men and women together. All the people I met here had fallen victim to robbers in the desert. No one had the means to travel on to Algiers or Oran. Everyone had to hire themselves out somehow in order to earn a little money. Every morning we went to Place Tchad, where the Algerians would come looking for laborers for their construction sites or for the plantations.

If you got a construction job, as I did, you could count yourself lucky, because you slept and ate on the building site. However, the conditions we worked in were tantamount to slavery. We were assigned to demolish old buildings or carry sacks of cement, were constantly told to work faster, and worked extremely hard, all too often for ridiculously low pay. Sometimes we had to empty toilets in the most unhygienic of conditions. We were denied any possibility of demanding our rights. If you spoke up, you were liable to be threatened by your boss, who usually would not hesitate to call the police over the smallest thing. Our working conditions were so harsh that if the police did suddenly appear, we lacked the strength to flee. Sometimes, after we had done the work, our bosses simply withheld our wages and threatened to call the police on us.

However, Place Tchad was also a meeting place for migrants. Every day we gathered there to talk. Each group gave an account of the route they had taken and the suffering they had endured. We discovered that the experiences of those who had traveled through Niger and through Mali respectively were very similar.

Everyone who told their story ended it with the words, "If I ever get to Algiers, I'm going to advise everyone not to take this route."

After telling each other what had happened to us on the road, we usually discussed political issues. Here, too, I heard what I'd already heard at many other points on my journey. People complained about the maladministration of their homelands and described how politicians there robbed their countrymen and worked solely in the interest of their own families. We also compared Africa's riches with those of the rest of the world. All those who spoke would mention the tremendous riches of the DRC and the fact that this country alone was capable of feeding the whole of Africa. Our Malian friends were always surprised that "Zaireans," as they called us, had had to go into exile, because they knew nothing about war or political persecution in Mali at that time; they were among those seeking a better life. But there were also travelers from the DRC who had left the country for economic or personal reasons. Some women told us they were following their husbands, who were already living in Europe; the consulates had refused to issue visas for wives. I met people from Liberia and Côte d'Ivoire who had left because of the war, and who told me how they had only just escaped death. However, most of the people I met in Tamanrasset had left their country because of financial difficulties, and because they could see no future for themselves at home.

On Place Tchad, then, we discussed politics, economics, culture, and religion. We even developed ideas as to how our countries should be ruled so that their riches would be accessible to all. Some people intended to return home after their travels, to build factories or farm the land. One young migrant told us he planned to return to his homeland after his travels and establish a company there. However, he had sworn to himself that he wouldn't pay taxes, because they just went straight into the pockets of the people in power.

Everyone had his or her own "project." Some declared that they would take any work they could get in Europe: in the fields, on the roads, even in morgues. All that mattered was raising enough capital to be able to invest it back home. Others took a different view, saying they only wanted to work to support their parents. Investing in Africa was too risky, they said; you could lose everything overnight, as a result of looting or war. They supported their argument by pointing to all the African potentates who had transferred their riches abroad, and listed the villas, castles, and bank accounts their countries' presidents owned in this or that European country.

And when I saw, once again, that everyone had his or her own reasons for making this journey, that everyone was pursuing his or her own goal, I realized what mine was. I wanted to make Europeans understand the consequences of European support for so many African dictators.

Place Tchad was not just a locus for debate, though. It was also a place where we were hunted down. The police were liable to show up at any time, and anyone who was caught was sent back to Tinzaouten. However, the choice of square was strategic—it was difficult for police jeeps to access, and by the time they got in, the illegalized migrants would often manage to disappear.

| DEPARTURE FOR ALGIERS

One day, however, the police carried out a big raid in which they succeeded in arresting a large number of migrants and sending them back to Tinzaouten. A lot of construction sites were tar-

geted, whereas those working in the fields mostly escaped de-
tection. I was extremely lucky: the site I was working on at the
time wasn't raided. After this, a friend with whom I had traveled
to Mali, and who I had helped to get Malian papers, called his
brother in Europe and asked him for financial assistance to enable him to travel on to Algiers. The brother sent €200, and my
friend asked me if I wanted to go with him.

We made all our preparations for departure. Our travel coordinator bought the tickets at the bus station. There were twenty
in our group, and the coordinator divided us into two groups of
ten. One was to travel to Oran, the other to Algiers. I was put in
the second group. That night, we were brought to the house of
a Cameroonian who lived right beside the bus station, and we
spent the night at his place. The next morning, each of us had to
pay him a fee. We went to the bus station at 4:00 a.m. to catch
the first bus. A lot of people were already waiting, and they all
stared at us. We already had our tickets and were able to board
the designated bus—but then our departure was delayed until
a police jeep showed up around 6:00 a.m. We all had to disem-
bark again, and our papers were checked. All of us had Malian
passports and visas; we'd organized that in Tinzaouten. Nonetheless, the police were clearly intending to make problems for
us. Our travel coordinator had told us that, if this happened, we
should whisper to the policeman, "Moi, j'ai le café." So we did—
whereupon the policemen escorted us to one of their jeeps. Same
old game: we were asked to pay up. Some gave one hundred di-
nars, others two hundred. After this we were brought back to the
bus, and it was able to depart a few minutes later. It had become
clear to me that police all over Africa follow the same procedure.

———

We were on the road for almost three days, and passed several roadblocks along the way. At some of them it was enough just to show our passports; at others we had to bribe the policemen again. Three of our traveling companions were arrested—they were from Niger, and the visas they'd been issued in the Nigerien town of Arlit were clearly invalid. No amount of pleading was of any use; they were taken away and deported.

When we drew into the bus station in Algiers, I was over-joyed. I thought that this was the end of my ordeal and I would be able to live here in peace. But when I reached the migrant ghetto in the district of Dely Ibrahim, all my hopes were dashed. Never at any point in my journey had I thought that, in a big city like Algiers, people might live in such wretched conditions. No-where in Africa had I ever seen people forced to live in the woods, sleeping in the undergrowth. I had to come to the capital of Al-geria to see this with my own eyes. We had finally arrived, weary and exhausted, and now there wasn't even a place for us to rest.

At around 7:00 p.m., some young people showed up at the ghetto. I asked them where they had come from, and they an-swered that they were returning from work. They had brought mineral water, juice, bread, yogurt, and other food. The quality of these provisions gave me hope—in the DRC, only the bour-geoisie and people on the fringes of power would have been able to afford such items. I soon learned why migrants were forced to sleep out in the open: in Algiers, it was forbidden for people with no papers—the sans-papiers—to rent a house. Any sans-papiers who dared to do so would end up in jail.

Algiers takes pride in its buildings and freeways, yet migrants are forced to sleep in the open. They hide in the woods and waste-lands of the city, but the police know exactly where they are.

And so my arrival in Algeria was just the start of an ordeal far worse than anything I had experienced in Cameroon, Benin, or Mali. In those countries, it was hard for the authorities to tell who was a local and who wasn't, who had papers and who didn't. Here, our skin color betrayed us from afar.

I spent the first night lying on a simple sack under a blanket given to me by a friend. I'd gotten used to living like this over the course of my journey. What shocked me was the fact that the buildings and streets here were in such good shape, yet we were forced to live in terrible conditions, and not for lack of money, but because we were sans-papiers.

In Algeria, if you have no papers, you have no worth, no dignity, and no rights. Yet Algeria, too, is a country of emigration— its people are drawn to Europe. Sub-Saharan migrants serve as scapegoats. Pointing the finger at us makes it possible to obscure the fact that Algerian citizens also take the route of illegal emigration, whether for political or for economic reasons. Sub-Saharans are vilified; they are abused, subjected to racist rebuffs, and exploited at the same time. Algeria receives political and economic dividends for "managing" sub-Saharan migrants: the EU pays the Maghreb countries to act as Europe's guard dogs.

During my stay in this country, my impression was that Algerians had no respect whatsoever for sub-Saharan migrants. Even little children saw us as worthless. They were already used to seeing the police hunt us down, tie us up, bundle us into trucks, and lock us behind bars. Whenever they spotted us, they shouted, "Hey, pal, where's your passport?" We were seen as beggars, unintelligent and uneducated.

This contempt was also apparent at hospitals. If you were sick and asked for medical assistance, the police would likely be called. People were taken away without being treated. The entire population rejected us and looked down on us. We were only regarded as useful if we were doing hard physical labor—that is, if we could be economically exploited. On the streets of Algiers, especially in the poorer districts, people insulted us, calling us "azzi"—slaves—and sometimes throwing stones at us. I was both a victim of and a witness to numerous such attacks, the likes of which I'd thought belonged to a bygone era when Arabs used to trade in Black slaves. Yet these humiliating practices still existed—slavery and dehumanization were not a thing of the past. It was inconceivable to me that young Algerians in particular, boys and girls who, like us, were potential emigrants and wanted to go to Europe, could show such racism toward us. The racist discourse was also fueled by the Algerian press, which painted an exclusively negative picture of sub-Saharan migrants.

During my work with ARCOM (see chapter 5), I would learn that the inhumane treatment to which we undocumented sub-Saharans were subjected in all the Maghreb countries immediately got worse whenever Europe increased pressure on the border. The EU uses the North African countries to enforce its migration policy. The externalization of the EU's border policy thus results in migrants dying unnatural deaths in the desert or at sea. The policy also reinforces racism and xenophobia and poisons relations between peoples. Europe gives the North African countries substantial political and economic support toward closing the borders, even though it's clear that these countries are often violating human rights. As I was revising the second German edition of this book, in April 2015, the terrible images of the boat disasters in the Mediterranean were being broadcast

around the world.* People were also seeing footage document-
ing the inhumane treatment of migrants imprisoned in transit
camps. All are direct consequences of the policy of closing and
further externalizing the EU's borders. Rather than relent, Europe continues to intensify these strategies, apparently in the
belief that this is the way to eradicate the problem of so-called
"illegal" immigration. But these methods don't solve the problem; they simply displace it.

The intensification of migratory movements from Africa that
we are seeing today exposes a long-concealed chaos. Africa was
made poor by multinational businesses and international financial institutions, like the International Monetary Fund and the
World Bank, that imposed their structural adjustment programs
on the continent. The support given by Western countries to
African dictatorships and the armed conflicts they skillfully in-
cited so they could continue to plunder the continent's natural
resources on a grand scale—all of this is reflected in the boat
disasters.

| RAIDS, DEPORTATIONS, AND AN UNEXPECTED
OPPORTUNITY

All migrants in Algiers were constantly on their guard against
raids and the accompanying deportations. Sub-Saharan migrants seldom moved freely around the city; to do so was to risk
being arrested and packed off into the desert. Only women and

---

*On April 14, 2015, more than seven hundred people died when a
boat capsized about 70 miles off the Libyan coast.

babies were spared—but the women frequently had to pay a high price. The police would raid the ghetto during the day, and at night these same policemen extorted sexual services from the women, under threat of deportation. The women were defenseless; they knew only too well how hard it would be to get back to Algiers if they were deported.

As a rule, migrants who fell into the clutches of the police were imprisoned without trial, and sometimes endured more than four months behind bars before finally being deported. Under the Algerian system, they were transferred from one prison to another until eventually they were brought to Tamanrasset, and from there deported to Chibriche on the Algerian-Malian border.

The conditions in Algerian prisons were appalling. A friend who was detained for three months before being deported to Tinzaouten told us: "You're locked up in a cell with criminals, bandits, drug smugglers, and other offenders. The inmates—who are mostly Algerians—torture and rape the other inmates. They inflict every imaginable atrocity on us. Every time you get to a new prison, you're seen as a newcomer again and put through the same hell as before."

Two months had passed since I had first arrived at the little woodland, which was known as Zala. We were constantly hunted by the police. One day, at around 1:00 p.m., a friend who knew the area well invited me to go with him for a meal. He left me on my own after a little while and moved on to another restaurant. It was important to take such precautions, because the police were more likely to notice you if you went about in pairs or groups. In the restaurant there was a young Malian woman who was watching me. After a while she came over and asked if I would like a fruit juice. I accepted. We shared the juice and started chatting. She asked me where I lived, and when I said I was living in Dely Ibrahim, she exclaimed, "But you seem like an educated man—only illegals live in Dely Ibrahim! You can't stay there!" I explained to her how I had come to Algeria, and she realized that I was no different from any of the others living in that part of town. She asked me if I had studied, and I told her I'd been in the final year of an economics degree at the University of Mbuji-Mayi in the DRC. By now she looked completely confused—my biography did not correspond to her idea of an illegal migrant. Like most Africans who go abroad to study, she had a very negative image of migrants. You have to be from a rich family in order to study abroad. Only the wealthy succeed in accessing scholarships.

We sat for a while without speaking. The young woman said again that Dely Ibrahim was not a good place for me. She suggested that she could put me in touch with Congolese students in the city. I agreed, so we took a taxi to the city center. She sat down with me in a café, ordered something for me, and went away. An hour later she returned with a Congolese man from Brazzaville, who said I could go with him to the campus of the University of Science and Technology at Bab Ezzouar. Once again the young Malian woman, Fatou, paid for a taxi, and we drove off. At the university I was met by two very nice young students, Ernest and Chris. We immediately got along, and they suggested I come and stay with them.

And so that night I slept indoors for the first time since arriving in Algeria.

I would like to take this opportunity to thank Fatou from the bottom of my heart for introducing me to these students. I'm also deeply grateful to these two friends, who let me stay with them for the next two months.

Living on the university campus was great for me, but when October came I couldn't keep staying with my friends there any longer. The semester had begun, and the authorities were conducting checks all over the campus. I was becoming more and more of a risk for them, and they couldn't think of a solution. I suggested that I leave and go back to Dely Ibrahim so they wouldn't get into trouble, but they wouldn't hear of it. Another Congolese student, whom I'd gotten to know on campus and who shared my political convictions, suggested I go to Morocco. I agreed to this, so he called the chairman in Dely Ibrahim. He was the one who would arrange my journey.

| DEPARTURE FOR MOROCCO

The journey from Algeria to Morocco was nowhere near as easy as one might expect. It called for absolutely meticulous preparation. First of all, I had to wait until the chairman had put together a convoy. At least four people had to register for the journey. As elsewhere, the chairman here in Algiers was himself a migrant who for some reason wasn't able to continue his journey, and so specialized in helping new arrivals travel on to Morocco in order to earn the money to do the same. He was in direct contact with the other chairmen in Morocco—in Maghnia, in Oujda, even in the woods of Bel Younech*—so he had all the necessary information at his fingertips.

*Bel Younech borders the Spanish exclave of Ceuta. Many migrants try to enter Europe from here.

One Sunday, at around 9:00 p.m., the chairman came to take me to Dely Ibrahim. We would be setting off from there. At 4:30 a.m. a taxi brought us to the Algiers train station. In our group we were three Congolese men and one Nigerian. We took nothing with us other than the absolute essentials; I had to leave behind the clothes that I'd bought so as not to stand out on the university campus. We were told to bring a coat and a pair of slip-on shoes, as well as a backpack with bread, yogurt, and other food.

Alain, one of the men from the DRC, had grown up in Kinshasa, but he had family connections to my home region; we even had a few acquaintances in common. Alain had embarked on his journey at the age of fourteen, shortly after his father died, and had now just turned nineteen. The poor boy was utterly traumatized by his terrible experience of trying to cross the desert. He had been deported back to Tinzaouten three times since arriving in Algeria. The suffering he had endured had left its mark. I'd met him in Algiers; he'd been in a really terrible state, so I had decided to help him and had advanced him a large part of the travel money.

We boarded the train to Oran with our travel coordinator. The train journey was scheduled to take eight hours, and it went off without a hitch. We got to Oran station undetected. Our chairman in Algiers called a taxi driver who was supposed to take us from Oran to Maghnia, the town on the Moroccan border. The taxi driver came, but he wasn't prepared to take us before 6:00 p.m. because it was Ramadan, the fasting month. He told us to wait in a hotel, but my three fellow travelers didn't have enough money for that. We were in a tricky situation. The taxi driver was starting to get nervous, and out on the street we risked being arrested by the police. Eventually we persuaded him to drive us to a woodland on the outskirts of Oran. We would hide there and wait for him until evening. The driver insisted we lie down on the ground so we wouldn't be spotted by the police helicopters searching the area for terrorists. This was not the kind of woods you might find in northern Europe, with tall trees and thick undergrowth. We were more or less in the desert; the trees here were small, and provided scarcely any shelter. The helicopters were circling above us. We were terribly afraid, as well as hungry and thirsty. Although we had bought bread and juice on our arrival in the town, we didn't dare eat or drink. For three hours we lay motionless, waiting. I was revisited by painful memories of the journey across the Sahara. Here we were yet again, completely helpless and exposed to all manner of dangers.

Fortunately, our driver's car eventually appeared. He honked the horn, and we rushed over and got in. After fifteen kilometers we met up at a gas station with a second taxi carrying several Malians, and the two vehicles traveled on in convoy. On the way, our driver, who must have been about fifty, told us he had been working as a trafficker between Algeria and Morocco for fifteen years and had a lot of experience in this profession. "I've brought a lot of African friends to Maghnia," he said. "Some of them have already gotten to Europe; they call me from time to time. I usually work with my colleague in the second car. He's also a decent man, and has never left travelers in the lurch." Our driver was telling the truth. Later, when I got to Rabat, I discovered that all my friends there knew him, and he had a good reputation with them.

And so we headed toward Morocco. Our driver told us to follow his instructions to the letter. If he stopped the car and said the words "Camarade Aya Aya," we were to jump out and hide as quickly as possible. During the drive, he often spoke on the phone with the other driver leading our little convoy. It was his job to let us know if we were in danger. Our driver had good contacts, so we got through several police checkpoints without any problems. At one of them, though, the police refused to let us pass. Here, too, our driver knew the officers, but we were obliged to get out nonetheless. They said we had to wait for a patrol car, which would take us to the police station. It was only after the police officers and our driver had a long discussion in Arabic that they let us drive on. Once we were under way again, our driver said he had made promises to the police officers that he didn't intend to keep.

We arrived in Maghnia at around 10:00 p.m. Our driver called another driver, who was to take us to the Moroccan border. When he showed up, we were suddenly told that we each had to pay €20. Two of my fellow travelers refused, saying that the chairman in Algiers had not mentioned this charge. The driver refused to back down. He started to threaten us; we were in serious danger of being turned over to the police. We also knew that there were a lot of Algerian vagrants in Maghnia, and that they had violently attacked Black migrants. We cursed the chairman in Algiers, who hadn't given us the correct information. The Malians traveling with us knew about the toll; they paid, and traveled on. I tried in vain to persuade my two fellow travelers to pay as well. In the end, I agreed to lend them €40, and I paid the driver €60 for the three of us. We said goodbye to the driver who had brought us this far, changed cars, and drove to the Moroccan border.

All this happened on October 22, 2004. At 10:30 p.m., the driver suddenly stopped the car and ordered us to get out and quickly hide behind a house. It was already quite dark; we could hardly see the building. A few minutes later, we heard some young people arrive and start talking to the driver, and shortly afterward they called out to us. It turned out that these young people were sub-Saharans. They greeted us in Lingala, and began to explain to us how to cross the Moroccan border. They explained that the streetlamps on the Algerian side were white, whereas on the Moroccan side they were red. Then they gave us instructions about what we had to look out for while walking, and how we should behave if we were stopped by attackers, or the police.

And so we set off for Oujda. We walked one behind the other, accompanied by two of the sub-Saharans who had come to meet us. One walked in front, the other in the middle. No one said a word. Our footsteps were the only sound. From time to time, someone would fall and get up again. Many dangers lurk along the twelve kilometers that separate the two border towns—thorns, stones, potholes, but above all bandits, police patrols, and the dogs guarding the surrounding farmsteads. Three times we were attacked by packs of dogs. This was nothing new for our guides; they told us to arm ourselves with stones and use them to drive the dogs away. The final attack was horrendous. A dog followed us and attacked us even though we threw stones. I started shouting for help, even though that risked attracting the attention of police or bandits. Our guides were furious—they told us we were jeopardizing all our efforts in getting this far, and could be deported to Tinzaouten at any moment. That night I felt very close to death. It was quite cold, but we were sweating. Twice we heard gunshots. I found myself remembering the day the rebel troops of Laurent-Désiré Kabila, who saw himself as a liberator, arrived in Mbuji-Mayi. Every time shots were fired we had to throw ourselves to the ground and wait until our guides gave us the signal to carry on walking.

| OUJDA

We had been walking for two hours when we reached a spot in the woods where a car was waiting for us. We got in, and the driver raced off at top speed. He kept the headlights switched off so as not to attract the attention of the police. Twenty minutes later we arrived in Oujda. The streetlights we had seen from afar when we were about to set off were now right in front of us. Our two guides gave sighs of relief, and started to speak to us differently. They adopted a brotherly tone, and told us what had happened to them the previous week. The migrants they were supposed to lead across the border never arrived; they'd been told that they had disappeared. The Moroccan driver had forced them to pay the money he'd lost out on: 200 dirhams [$19] for each of the missing passengers.

Our two guides brought us to a building where a man— clearly their boss—was waiting for us. The two young men gave him their report, then they disappeared. We stayed in the house. The boss led us to a small room that already had about twenty people in it: migrants, like us. He called us up one after another. We had to state where we were from and what route we had taken. Afterward, he drummed into us that this was a transit station and we had to travel on to Rabat the next day. He explained the travel arrangements to us, and named the price we had to pay. I was shocked by this enormous sum and tried to negotiate with him, but there was nothing to be done about it; the man even started threatening me, saying his henchmen would beat me up if I didn't do as I was told. I had no option but to pay. This meant that, although up until now I'd been supporting our youngest fellow traveler, Alain, financially, I was no longer able to advance him enough money to cover his travel expenses. Was he now going to get stuck here in Oujda? I was very worried about my young friend. What could I do to prevent him from being deported again? I couldn't think of a solution. All I was able to do was give Alain what little money I had left; he had to stay behind in Oujda.

Later, I heard that the boss's apartment had been raided by the police. The boss was arrested and the other migrants deported to the border. I was worried about what had happened to Alain, but he made it to Rabat after all, a few weeks after us, and was able to tell me in person about his ordeal in Oujda.

Now, though, we spent another night in the wretched accommodation our contact person had provided before embarking on our journey to Rabat. We were all hungry and exhausted from the long walk across the border. I took a shower; the water was icy. There was nothing to eat. We had to lie on bare concrete, without mattresses or blankets. At around 3:00 a.m. I started shivering uncontrollably. I thought my time was up. But God protected me, and I survived this dreadful night as well.

I woke very early the following morning. Not because we were leaving, but because I was so hungry I couldn't sleep. Only those the boss trusted were allowed to leave the room; everyone else was locked in. The people who were allowed out bought clothes and food for the rest of us.

We talked. I found out that some people had been here for

weeks because they didn't have the money to travel on. I was especially touched by the fate of one of my fellow Congolese. Kelor had been stuck there for three months, had lost all contact with his family, and was surviving on the generosity of other travelers, who occasionally slipped him twenty or thirty dirhams. Things were especially difficult for him, because he walked with a limp. He asked me to contact his parents by e-mail and explain his situation to them, which I did when I got to Rabat. Six months later, he made it there, too. Like so many others, Kelor planned to make the crossing to Europe, and made for the border between Morocco and the Spanish enclave of Ceuta. He was living in the woods of Bel Younech, just outside the Spanish city, but when the police raids there intensified, he decided to go to Libya and brave the crossing to Italy from there. Later, we heard from our Congolese friends in Libya that the boat he was on had capsized, and he had drowned. Dead—after all the torments he had endured, far from his parents, who may never even have heard what happened to him. May his soul rest in peace!

At around 6:00 p.m., the boss called me to him, explained how to get to the station, and gave me the final instructions for the journey. Before I left, he also whispered to me that I would see a Congolese woman with three children at the station—I should keep a close eye on her, be wary of her, and not approach her, or I might end up being deported.

I took a taxi and arrived at the station ten minutes before the train was due to depart. I went to the ticket desk and, sure enough, there was the woman with the three children. She spoke to me in Lingala and said her name was Brigitte. She asked me to help her, because she wasn't allowed to buy a ticket to Rabat. I was terribly afraid that she really was working for the police and might turn me in, so I didn't reply. I was afraid they wouldn't let me buy a ticket either, but my fears were unfounded. I took the ticket, and without paying any further attention to the Congolese woman or her children I walked to the train, where all the passengers were being checked by the police. I showed them the residence permit that the boss of our "network" had given me less than twenty-four hours earlier, and I was allowed to board the train. From there I glanced back at the ticket counter and saw Brigitte weeping, begging for a ticket. It broke my heart. When the children started crying as well, she was suddenly sold a ticket. She came running to the train; and now, strangely, the police no longer had time to check her papers. Despite all these very peculiar circumstances, I couldn't help myself; I ran to the door to help her and the children board the train. I found her a seat in another compartment, then returned to mine.

I have no way of knowing whether the events on that journey had anything to do with Brigitte. Either way: I was checked by the police four times. During one of the checks I thought I was going to be deported at any minute. The officers doubted the validity of my residence permit and demanded to see my passport. Of course, I had no passport to show them, but after a half-hour discussion, they allowed me to continue my journey after all.

| OCTOBER 24, 2004—ARRIVAL IN RABAT

The train arrived in Rabat at 6:00 a.m. I went to the taxi rank, heading for a part of town called Hay Nahda, as the people in Oujda had suggested. Brigitte was still following me. She kept talking to me, asking if I could help her travel on. I knew I'd already taken a risk by helping her in Oujda, so I acted as if I hadn't heard her. I hurried to my taxi and got out of there.

When we were on the way, I asked the taxi driver if I could borrow his cell phone. I called Abdoul, the Congolese contact person whose name I'd been given. He answered the call, and promised to pick me up at the agreed-upon place.

The apartment he brought me to consisted of three rooms with more than fifteen people living in them. I was shown to a room that already had seven people in it: four teenage boys, two women in their late twenties, and another woman of about forty. In the next room, a pregnant woman and her husband were billeted with three young guys; five more men lived in the third room. I lay down to sleep and didn't wake until about 1:00 p.m.

When I got up, my new roommates cross-examined me about my journey. They wanted to hear every detail. Mostly I told them about my experiences in Oujda, also mentioning my encounter with Brigitte. We discovered that we had had very similar experiences on the train. It had been particularly bad for one of the teenage migrants: the police had arrested him on the train, thrown him into jail, and deported him to Maghnia, where he was attacked and robbed of everything he owned.

The middle-aged woman told me about life in Rabat. There was no work for migrants; people lived from "the ten numbers," a reference to Western Union transfer codes. Anyone who didn't have relatives or friends sending them money from Europe or from home was destitute. Life here was very hard, my roommates said; you had to be extremely frugal. They also advised me not to leave the house more than absolutely necessary, as there was a high risk of being stopped by the police and deported.

The woman spent all day praying in our room. She was a Christian, but she observed Ramadan as well. She had lost contact with her husband along the way, and hoped that if she did this, she might appease God and find her husband again.

After just two days, the apartment and the people living there were making me feel terribly depressed. One of the men who shared my room—a boxer—noticed my low mood; he suggested I move to a different place nearby, where I might be happier. No sooner said than done. The next day, I switched to another apartment that also had three rooms, but far fewer inhabitants. There were several young men living there, and a woman with her two-year-old son; she had no money to pay the rent, and was supported by the other occupants. It was very quiet there. People stayed at home during the day, and spent the time praying. Everyone in the house was Christian. Most didn't get up until after midday. The rule was that if you left the apartment, you had to get away from the house as fast as possible, so as not to attract the police's attention to the community.

I shared a room with a boy whose leg was in a cast. He told me he had tried to get to Spain, but had been deported back to Morocco after taking the ferry to Algeciras. In Tangier they had locked him in a cell, then sent him back to the Algerian border. From there he had headed to the Mediterranean again, and had gotten as far as the woods of Bel Younech. He told me he had planned to scale the fence separating Morocco from Ceuta, but the situation had become increasingly difficult. In order to risk this dangerous border crossing, you had to wait weeks, months, even years for a suitable opportunity to present itself. You also had to be equipped to deal with life in the woods; you needed nerves of steel. After a few weeks, the boy—his name was Bay—had decided to leave Bel Younech and go back to Rabat, but on his way there he was attacked by Moroccan vagrants. They broke his leg and stole all his possessions. The villagers who found him after the attack contacted Doctors Without Borders, who helped arrange for him to be taken to a hospital in Rabat. Many lives have been saved by the help Doctors Without Borders has provided to illegalized migrants.

C ontrary to what my friend in Algiers had promised, my
situation did not improve in the slightest when I got to
Rabat. In fact, my life there proved even harder. As a
migrant in Algiers, you could at least find illegal work on construction sites, doing removals, loading and unloading goods, or
other odd jobs, some reasonably paid, some not. There was none
of this in Rabat. Migrants were not allowed to work. The people
they referred to as "Africans"—as if Morocco weren't also part
of Africa—were discriminated against in all areas of public life.
Property owners here did accept sub-Saharan tenants, which
was not the norm in Algiers, but our status was still extremely
insecure.

| LIVING CONDITIONS

Generally speaking, renting a house or apartment in Rabat was
easy, especially in the working-class districts. The downside of
this was that migrants were charged much higher rents than

local people for equivalent apartments. As a result, we were forced to band together in groups. Ten people would often share an apartment with only two rooms; there were fifteen men in my apartment. The cramped housing conditions were not without consequences. Women and girls were subjected to sexual assault; there were cases of women being abused by members of their own community, of unwanted pregnancies and abortions. Landlords often extorted sexual services from women who couldn't afford the rent, reducing them to the status of unwilling prostitutes. Many underage and defenseless women were pressured into this situation. There were a lot of underage mothers. They were even more hopelessly enslaved than the others, as they were usually even less able to provide for themselves and their children. This already dreadful situation was compounded by the fact that migrants had to live in terribly unhygienic conditions, and so were highly at risk of becoming infected with sexually transmitted diseases or tuberculosis.

The woman who lived with her child in the apartment I'd moved to was one of many migrant women who had been forced into prostitution. She and her daughter had a room to themselves, but paid the same rent as the other migrants who shared six to a room. In exchange, however, she was sexually controlled by an older migrant who was regarded as the apartment's chairman. One day, when she refused to do what she was told, he threw her out.

I was especially moved by the story of Octavie, an underage migrant I met in Rabat. She came looking for me one day. I could tell from her face that something terrible had happened to her. The torments she had suffered prompted her to confide in me things that, under normal circumstances, no African girl would ever tell any man. Like many others, she called me "Papa

Emman." She said: "Please help me find somewhere else to sleep. I have to share the room with five boys. I can't stand it there anymore; they harass me every night." I tried to find something for her, but I didn't succeed. After just a few months this young woman became pregnant. We didn't know who the father was, but I am certain it was one of her five roommates.

| ACCESS TO HEALTH CARE

In Morocco, migrants without papers were systematically denied access to the city's hospitals. The supposed justification for this was that if sans-papiers received treatment, immigration would only increase. This stance cost many people their lives. At one point while I was in Rabat, twelve Congolese migrants died in the space of just two months.

It's especially important to me that I tell the story of Maman Marie Mfunyi here. I met her through Albert, a pastor who lived at my apartment. Marie Mfunyi was very sick—we never knew with what—but her husband, who lived with her, didn't dare take her to the hospital as neither of them had papers. I called Dr. Anaclet Kalonji, a Congolese doctor who had come to Morocco many years earlier to study. He was a remarkable man who always rendered invaluable services to sub-Saharan refugees and migrants, and was well-known among sub-Saharan immigrants of all nationalities. You could call him at any time of the day or night; he was all too aware of our situation.

Dr. Kalonji agreed to come. He examined the sick woman and promised us that she would be treated in the Hôpital des

Spécialités in Rabat. Thanks to our friend's intervention, everything there went well; preliminary tests were carried out, and Maman Marie was referred to another hospital. Here, too, Dr. Kalonji exerted his influence, and her test samples were sent to the laboratory. However, as soon as Dr. Kalonji left to return to his work, the problems began. We waited hours and hours for the lab results to come back. Suddenly, around midnight, a doctor showed up; he told us that the samples had disappeared and they would have to take new ones. This they did, but after another two hours a different doctor came and informed us, without explanation, that we and the patient would have to go to the Maternité des Orangers. We tried to negotiate, but there was nothing to be done. We had no choice but to follow their instructions. However, when we got to this hospital, they didn't even take us in—they simply chased us away. We called Dr. Kalonji again. He was outraged by what had happened, but not especially surprised.

What were we to do? It was a cold night, and we were standing by the side of the road. Maman Marie was crying and sobbing. "C'est parce que je suis Noir!" she said. *This is happening to me because I'm Black.*

I hadn't eaten anything since the morning, and I was completely demoralized. We tried to hail a taxi, but when they saw the state the sick woman was in, no one would take us. It was an hour before we managed to find someone to drive us home, and by the time we got to Marie's house it was four in the morning.

It wasn't for lack of money that Marie went untreated. It was because she had no papers.

We tried again the following day, with Dr. Kalonji, but the whole affair was to take a far more tragic turn than we could ever have imagined. Marie was in a critical condition; she was admitted to hospital at Dr. Kalonji's insistence, but discharged the following day without receiving proper care. A few days later, her husband died of a heart attack. The recent events had proven too much for him. After this, I put out an appeal to a number of charitable organizations, as well as via the e-mail list of Manifeste Euro-Africain. My initiative bore fruit, and Caritas, Médecins du Monde, and Comité d'Entraide Internationale made sure that Marie received proper treatment—but it was all in vain. She died a few days later. When I visited her for the last time, with my friend Jean-Baptiste, who was also a pastor, we prayed together. Marie said to me: "Papa Emman, thank you for everything. They told me you organized a funeral for my husband. When I die, please make sure that I, too, am buried with dignity."

The refusal to provide migrants with adequate health care was also what caused the death of young Tony Mbombo. This boy's tragic death put the whole of the migrant community in Rabat in a state of uproar. Aid organizations in Morocco and Europe and representatives of the UNHCR also expressed their shock, as did a great many journalists.

Tony was eight years old. He was an extremely intelligent boy, and attended the Caritas school in Rabat. His mother's refugee status was recognized by the UNHCR. One day, Tony was attacked by a Moroccan child in Sidi Moussa, a suburb of Rabat, and badly beaten up. He was taken to a Moroccan charity hospital, but the treatment he received there was so inadequate that over the following month his wounds became infected. A team of journalists from the Spanish TV channel TVE were researching the situation of migrants in Morocco; they came across Tony, and decided to help him. With Dr. Kalonji's assistance, they succeeded in getting a new appointment for him to be admitted to the hospital. Dr. Kalonji and the Spaniards brought Tony in for the planned operation. They were initially told that a simple surgical procedure was all that was required, and it would all be over in a quarter of an hour. However, it turned out that the doctors on duty were anything but well disposed toward Tony. The boy was very scared. He confided in Dr. Kalonji that they had whispered to him, in Arabic: "Just you wait. You're going to die." They had pointed at the Spaniards and said, "You aren't ill at all. You're faking it; you just want them to believe you're suffering." Dr. Kalonji stayed with Tony until he fell asleep at 11:30 p.m. After that, he left the hospital, because he believed the operation wouldn't be performed until the following day. He planned to come back the following morning to be present during the operation. But at 2:00 a.m. Dr. Kalonji's phone rang. It was Tony's mother. She told him that her son had died.

The boy had been taken into the operating room half an hour after Dr. Kalonji left the hospital. A few minutes later, he was brought back out into the corridor, where his mother was waiting. He wasn't moving, and at first she thought he was still under anesthesia. But Tony never woke up. We will never know what really happened in that operating room.

No one could believe what had happened. Tony's funeral was held in Rabat's Christian cemetery, where hundreds of people came to pay their last respects. No one could contain their tears. I clung to Dr. Kalonji's arm; we were both weeping. Our friend Astrid held Tony's mother back when, in her despair, she tried to throw herself into her son's grave. I even saw the head of the UNHCR mission in Morocco sobbing; he attended the funeral in person.

———

The deaths of the Congolese people mentioned here could only be brought to public attention because we organized. In the following chapter I will illustrate just how important organization was for us.

In addition to the two cases I've described here, there were many others that were never clarified—for example, the bodies of thirteen sub-Saharan migrants that were found in the morgue of a hospital in Casablanca. No one knew what had caused their deaths. We would never even have heard where their corpses were if the Moroccan organization AFVIC* hadn't let us know.

| SCHOOLING

Children from families that have fled to Morocco to escape war, persecution, or economic disaster are not permitted to attend the public schools there, because their parents have no papers. Even the children of recognized refugees or asylum seekers are denied access to schooling. Consequently, these children live in a state of great insecurity about their future. No child has chosen to be in this situation; no child has forced their parents to emigrate. Yet these children's fundamental right to education is contested, and they are excluded.

Only about fourteen kilometers separate Morocco from Europe, where countries and international institutions guarantee the rights of the child. As well as the Moroccan schools—public and private—there are also European educational institutions

---

*AFVIC (Association des Amis et Familles des Victimes de l'Immigration Clandestine) is an organization for the relatives of illegalized Moroccan migrants who lost their lives crossing to Europe.

in Morocco. The majority of these are under Spanish or French management. But the children of migrants have no access to these schools, either. This is a scandal.

One day I was invited by a Moroccan staff member at UNICEF to take part in an international colloquium on the subject of children's rights. I was planning to inform the participants about the situation of refugee children in Morocco—but I was refused entry to the venue.

There are often reports about how, in certain parts of the Muslim world, parents do not send their children to school. It happens in Afghanistan; it happens in Morocco, too. We hear how international organizations argue about the matter with parents or religious leaders. There is, however, comparatively little reporting on the fact that countless children of sub-Saharan migrants are systematically denied access to education.

| THE WORLD OF WORK

Sans-papiers and asylum seekers in Morocco have no access to paid work of any kind, even irregular. Although it is often claimed that there aren't enough positions on the Moroccan job market, the root of the problem is the illegalization of migrants.

While I was living in Morocco, the head of the UNHCR office there, Johannes van der Klaauw, organized a training program for refugees. In conjunction with Morocco's Fondation Orient-Occident, it offered courses in the fields of nursing care, hotel catering, and call center work. A number of French businesses with call centers in Morocco even intended to specialize in employing refugees who spoke good French and had completed this training. However, the Moroccan authorities thwarted their plans: the person in charge at the Fondation Orient-Occident said he had received the instruction that no one could be employed without a residence permit.

The lack of paid work had serious consequences for all refugees and migrants in Morocco. I survived by giving French lessons to Moroccan children in private houses—clandestine employment, of course—and through very occasional cash transfers from my family in the Congo. As usual, the situation had a particularly dire impact on women; the effective employment ban forced many of them to take up sex work.

I ASYLUM, RAIDS, AND DEPORTATIONS

The woman with the two-year-old child who lived in our apartment in Rabat was a recognized refugee; she had an ID card issued by the office of the UNHCR. A few weeks after my arrival, I asked her to go with me to the UNHCR headquarters, which at the time was in Casablanca. I also intended to apply for asylum.

We got up at dawn and took the bus to Casablanca. There were already about ten people waiting outside the UNHCR office. After a while, we were received by a man who simply asked us to write our names and phone numbers on a piece of paper. We were sent away again without any further information. Everyone was very disappointed, but responded passively and followed the procedure. We returned to Rabat without achieving anything. The money we'd spent on getting there had all been in vain. I'd even paid the travel costs for my housemate along with my own. What shocked us most of all, though, was the manner in which we were received. We hadn't been given a document we could use to prove that we had applied for asylum; nor did the UNHCR ever call us back. As a result, we were still at risk of arbitrary arrest.

Refugees and migrants in Morocco were in constant danger of being caught up in raids and deportations. For this reason, we were condemned to spend most of our time in our apartments and ghettos. We were effectively prisoners there.

In January 2005, there was a large-scale raid on all the parts of town where migrants lived, including G5, Hay Nahda 1 and 2, and Takkadoum. I remember the events of that day very clearly. The previous evening, I'd been invited over by Michaux and Sylvain, who had a small child. Our conversation mostly revolved around a TV program that had announced that the Spanish king would be visiting Morocco. A number of friends who were also there that evening thought the Spanish king was coming to take migrants back to Spain. His country needed workers, they said. Besides, Spain needed young people, because the population was aging and the young people didn't want to get married and have children anymore. We debated this topic for three hours, and one of those present, a Cameroonian whom everyone liked and respected, argued emphatically that lots of us would now be able to travel to Spain. Many of the migrants there that evening were in excellent spirits, optimistic that they would now be able to leave Morocco.

However, things turned out completely differently. That very night, at around 4:00 a.m., the Moroccan police, the royal gendarmerie, and police auxiliaries carried out a terrible raid. They went from house to house abducting men, women, children, and babies, and deporting them to Oujda on the Algerian border. It was winter, and bitterly cold. Our friend from Cameroon, who had been so convinced that the Spanish king's visit meant that good things were in store, was also deported.

That night, I was lucky. Our house was spared. Afterward, word got around that our place was safe, which meant that as soon as rumors started circulating that a raid might be imminent, many friends would come and seek refuge at our house.

Nonetheless, I was very afraid that one day the police would raid our building, too. I hadn't had a response from the UNHCR; what was I supposed to do? They'd promised to call us back, but we hadn't heard a thing. I prayed a lot during that time. We were forced to hide all day. We went to the market only at prearranged times. When we needed to catch a bit of sunlight, we would stick to places that were safe from the police. We called these places "tranquilos." Even these excursions we only dared make at the times when the police officers took their breaks.

| PRAYER CIRCLES

Migrant groups founded informal churches where they could pray by day and at night. Most Christian migrants remained true to their faith, even though there were a lot of missionaries who tried to take advantage of their misery and persuade them to convert to Islam. The services took place in the ghettos, mostly in apartments where religious leaders lived. These people were referred to as pastors, evangelists, sometimes even apostles. Often, these were titles that had been bestowed on them during their migration. In times of difficulty—when crossing a border, or during arrests and deportations to the desert—they had distinguished themselves with particular prescience. Someone who gathered his fellow travelers to pray together and ask for God's blessing was referred to as a pasteur or, in the Nigerian community, a "man of god."

The prayer meetings were held in great secrecy, as there had already been instances of arrests being made when house owners heard about the religious meetings. Sometimes they called the police because the meetings were Christian; sometimes it was simply that they wouldn't allow informal gatherings on their property.

There were two prayer circles in our house. The leader of one was called a priest, the other an evangelist. Both were of Congolese origin. Each had his own following, and they alternated the days they held Mass—one on even days, the other on odd ones. Nonetheless, there were tensions between the two religious leaders; there was clearly a rivalry for leadership of the community. In this respect, at least, Muslim migrants had an advantage, as they were able to attend the official religious institutions—there were a lot of mosques in the working-class districts of the city.

Despite the frictions in our apartment, these churches played an extremely important role, affirming not just the migrants' spiritual outlook but their moral and political ones, too. People in the churches encouraged each other every day not to lose hope. Migrants were strengthened in their resolve not to give in to prostitution, criminality, or theft, despite the great suffering they had to endure, but instead to practice charity and mutual solidarity.

When there were conflicts within a community, or between different communities, the religious leaders were often called upon to resolve the arguments and restore peace. In short, the churches acted as a kind of moral guardrail. Members of a particular church were integrated into their community and tried to live a good life so as not to bring their community into disrepute. As sub-Saharan migrants were also denied access to the Moroccan justice system, the churches often served as arbitrating bodies. Some conflicts that we were unable to resolve at our association were swiftly and permanently settled following a consultation with a priest.

However, the churches didn't only play an important moral role; they also provided material support to their members. The offertory money—little though it was—was administered by a cashier and used to support pregnant women, the sick, or people in difficult situations.

These organizational practices, in this form, were completely new. They were developed by people living in extreme poverty who, in spite of their troubles, had decided to steer clear of criminality. Unfortunately, these innovative initiatives were never mentioned in the Moroccan press. If the papers did report on migrant religious associations, it was only ever in a negative way, and in order to criminalize us. A Moroccan weekly paper declared that American priests were funding sub-Saharan migrants to spread the Christian faith in Morocco. The article referred to the assistance provided by our American friend Pastor David Brown. But the migrants' precarious, informal churches existed completely independently of external support. They existed in Rabat, and in places like the woods outside the Spanish enclaves of Ceuta and Melilla. When they did receive support, the money never went to religious dignitaries but only to migrants in need, irrespective of their religion. Christian refugees were by no means the only ones who knocked on Pastor Brown's door; so did Muslims from Palestine, Iraq, and West Africa, as well as many migrants with no religious affiliation at all.

| CROSSING TO SPAIN

In December 2004, I received a call from a friend who lived in Rabat's G5 district. He told me that he had been contacted by someone who was organizing a crossing to Spain. They had agreed on a price of 6,000 dirhams [around $620] per person. My friend told me to spread the news in my area. One of my fellow travelers was interested—and I, too, wanted to attempt the crossing. I wanted to finally be able to live without having to stay hidden in one room. After so many years of suffering, I wanted to apply for asylum in Spain.

My first problem, though, was that I didn't have six thousand dirhams at my disposal. What should I do? The only thing I could think of was to call my big brother in the DRC. His initial response was negative—he didn't want me getting on a fishing boat under any circumstances. He had seen the terrible footage of shipwrecks on TV, and said it was definitely better to stay in Morocco than to die in the Mediterranean. I argued against this, saying that many people had made the crossing to Spain successfully; besides, I told him, here in Morocco I was in constant danger of being deported. If I stayed here any longer, one of these days I would end up in the desert. After a long discussion, I managed to convince him, and he transferred the money I needed via Western Union the following day.

We prepared ourselves for the journey. I bought gloves, a coat, a hat, and food supplies. My friend said goodbye to his wife, who was staying behind with their baby. They said their farewells in the hope of seeing each other again in Spain. That was the rule: if a good opportunity presented itself, you let your loved ones go and hoped that you would see them again one day.

At around 5:00 p.m. I finished my shopping and went home to eat and say goodbye to my housemates. I had arranged to meet the friend I was traveling with at 8:00 p.m. A chairman was supposed to come and lead us to a tranquilo. From there we would be taken to Nador, where the crossing was to begin.

My friend showed up punctually at 8:00 p.m., accompanied by the chairman, who demanded that I give him the travel money right away. I hesitated, and said I would only hand over the money when we got to the tranquilo. In the end, I prevailed. We said a short prayer and set off. Just ten minutes later we came to a house where more than twenty people were already waiting. Each was carrying a small backpack, as was I. Some had already been waiting in this dump for two days, some for as long as five days, without being allowed even to step outside the house. The rules really were extremely strict: the boss of our "network" immediately started lecturing my friend, because he had violated the rules by leaving the house to fetch me. Things didn't calm down until some time later. The boss brought food: foufou,* smida,† and chicken. Everybody ate; I was the only one with no appetite. From the moment I'd set foot in this tranquilo I'd started to regret setting off on this adventure.

Sure enough, at around 10:00 p.m. the trouble began. The landlord of the apartment, who lived above us, suddenly turned up and started shouting. He hadn't been told that there were so

---

*A thick mash of manioc, or yams, and plantains.
†Semolina.

many of us, he said; he'd rented the apartment to just six people. He shouted and shouted, demanding to know who we were and what we were doing there. Of course, he also saw that there weren't enough foam mattresses in the room, and that all we had with us were backpacks. Eventually he called his wife and children, who also started yelling. Our hiding place was in danger of being discovered. The owner of the apartment ordered the boss of our network to get hold of the smuggler he had rented the apartment to and make him come over. The man didn't exactly live close by, though, so it was a while before he finally showed up. After some tough negotiation, the landlord and the smuggler reached an agreement. Each person there would have to pay twenty-five dirhams. The situation was serious, as the landlord was threatening to call the police if we didn't pay up. We were feeling increasingly insecure at this location. As we Congolese migrants used to say, "Ndaku esumbi"—the house had become uninhabitable. Despite the impending danger, the majority of the migrants refused to give in to the landlord's attempts at blackmail, so the smuggler was forced to evacuate us and look for a different place. He promised the landlord he would pay the amount he was demanding later on, out of his own pocket. Meanwhile, we were ordered to leave the apartment in groups of two.

By the following day, the smuggler had organized a new "network" apartment—but there was a nasty surprise in store for me and my traveling companion. We, along with all the Congolese travelers, were refused entry. My friend was accused of attracting the landlord's attention with his careless behavior. And so we stayed behind in Morocco.

However, as it turned out, the fact that we were not allowed to make the crossing was our salvation. Four days later we saw the bodies of our Malian and Guinean friends on television. All of them had died in a shipwreck. When I saw the footage, the events of all the preceding weeks flashed through my mind. I thought of the long discussions I'd had with my brother. I remembered how I'd refused to give the chairman the money for the crossing, promising to give it to him afterward instead. And I relived my unease on arriving at the tranquilo.

But it wasn't just these memories that tormented me. I also relived the whole of my odyssey from Mali to Morocco. After all that, I had come within a hair's breadth of dying at sea. It was sheer chance that had saved me.

That day I decided to go back to the headquarters of the UNHCR in Casablanca and apply for asylum in Morocco. I was determined to remind the person responsible—the one who had turned us away last time—of his promise. Whatever happened, I wanted to get protection in Morocco until the situation in the DRC had normalized.

Still in need of a way in, I had to search for new opportunities. With the help of a friend, who was also a migrant but who, unlike me, had a residence permit, I managed to start a computer science training course. Officially, it was my friend who was registered for the course; as a sans-papiers I wouldn't have stood a chance of being accepted.

| ASYLUM SEEKERS IN MOROCCO

I didn't know it then, but my story with the UNHCR was only just beginning. In March 2005, we were informed that the

UNHCR was opening an office in Rabat. Early the very next day we sent a small delegation to the site of the High Commissioner's new office to check if what we'd been told was true. Indeed—the information had been accurate. The office was staffed, and my roommates and I even got an appointment for the following day.

We could only go into the center of the city if we were well-dressed and could pass as students; it was advisable to carry pens and a briefcase. Otherwise, you risked arrest. Even going to our first appointment at the UNHCR office, we had to walk past several police officers in their patrol cars. Fortunately, we weren't stopped and checked. After an initial conversation we were asked to come in for individual appointments, at which we would be interviewed. My appointment was on March 18. By then, others had already had their interviews and were waiting for their asylum applications to be confirmed. On the day itself, everything suddenly happened very fast. A member of the UNHCR staff interviewed me for more than an hour about my migration history. Then he photographed me. Ten minutes later, I was holding my asylum application in my hands. I was beside myself with joy. Several other friends had also had their applications confirmed. We went home and had a big celebration.

I thought that having the paper from the UNHCR would end my life of seclusion. How wrong I was. No work was to be had without regular resident status. I made this bitter discovery when, with the help of a student from Brazzaville, I applied for a job at a call center that was employing sub-Saharan migrants who spoke good French. I drew up a letter of application and a CV and, accompanied by my friend, took these documents to the call center office. I even received a phone call three days later, and was asked about my application. The interview would have gone well if the company employee hadn't asked me at the end of it about my status in Morocco. I answered that I was registered with the UNHCR as an asylum seeker. I was devastated by her response: they could only employ migrants with an official Moroccan residence permit. I persisted, and the woman promised to call me back. When I didn't hear from her, I decided to pay another visit to the call center—but when I got there, they simply confirmed that my job application had been rejected. All my hopes evaporated. This avenue was closed to me.

I had thought the UNHCR paper would protect me from arrest and deportation, but that was a huge mistake as well. Although the UNHCR now had an office in Rabat, the raids on sans-papiers continued. Everyone was affected, including those who could prove they had made an asylum application, or were even recognized refugees.

At the end of 2005, there was another large-scale raid in a district with a large migrant population. All those who were picked up were deported, in inhumane conditions, to Oujda. People who believed they had the right to remain because they had the UNHCR paper, and who tried to defend themselves, were brutally mistreated. I remember one asylum seeker who had given birth two weeks earlier; she was shown no mercy, and was deported to Oujda along with her baby. From there she made many calls to the pastor with whom I shared an apartment, asking him to pray for her and the child. Calls reached us from other deportees as well, but in our situation there was nothing we could do for them.

In all this time, not one single nongovernmental organization dared to speak out in protest. Not even the UNHCR said a word. The few NGOs that worked with migrants were more concerned with those of us who were living in the woods on the outskirts of big cities. Other organizations, like Caritas, confined themselves to providing social support to those affected, and did not make political protests. The silence around the deportations encouraged the police, and the rounding up of sub-Saharan refugees and migrants continued.

5

FOUNDING ARCOM

I t took me a while to work out what to do next. Like countless other refugees living in Morocco, I was in a difficult
situation.

I found myself drawing inspiration from my former political
experience in the DRC. Back when I was a student in Mbuji-
Mayi, a fellow campaigner called Richard had given a speech
at the first conference of our political group. He concluded with
words that left a deep impression on me: "We have only two options. Either we betray our principles, or we fight."

Now, as then, we could choose one of two paths. Either we
could accept the injustices, the degrading treatment, the misery and suffering, the vilification to which we were constantly
exposed—or we could take our destiny into our own hands and
choose to fight, to push back against the discriminatory and xenophobic conduct of the police, the government, and the media.
This would also mean demanding that they adhere to international conventions. It would mean insisting that we were not the
victims of criminal structures and smugglers—that our problem
was repression, enacted by a government we had not elected, a

government that was not accountable to anyone for its actions. It would also mean drawing attention to the fact that we were victims of armed conflict, and that the only reason these conflicts were perpetuated was that the warring parties were fighting over the exploitation of natural resources—resources that could be used to secure our happiness and well-being and release us from our odyssey.

The answer was clear. But how were we to put all this into practice? Individual actions seemed wholly inadequate. Instead, we needed to create a framework, a structure, with which people could get involved, one that would strengthen mutual solidarity and facilitate communication.

At this time, the majority of the asylum seekers in Morocco were from the DRC. This could be attributed, on the one hand, to the political instability and armed conflicts that had wrecked the country. On the other hand, though, many Congolese men and women fled to Morocco because Mobutu, his family, and his political followers had found shelter there. Refugees from the DRC presented themselves at the UNHCR office in large numbers. People from other sub-Saharan countries—Côte d'Ivoire, for example—were less likely to take advantage of this opportunity. Generally speaking, one problem was that the majority of refugees and migrants kept to their own communities. Everyone mistrusted everyone else, and people lived in constant fear of being picked up and deported. We felt most secure among our own countrymen and -women, and were more inclined to trust them.

In the end, it was the sermons of Pastor Jon Ghéber that reinforced my decision to set up an organization for sans-papiers. "God has equipped us with great abilities, and it is up to us to apply them to changing our lives," he said in his sermon one Sunday. "Whatever situation we find ourselves in, let us pray to God to help us use all our capabilities. We cannot simply stand back and fold our arms. No—we must arise!"

After this service I went home with the feeling that my resolution had been approved. I had to arise and put an end to my isolation. I had to change not only my own life but the lives of my comrades living here with me in exile.

And so I founded ARCOM, the Association de réfugiés et demandeurs d'asile congolais au Maroc—the Association of Congolese Refugees and Asylum Seekers in Morocco. I created this association with the aim of encouraging the other communities to follow my example. Later on, some people were indeed inspired by this, and founded their own associations to defend the rights of their compatriots.

| THE FOUNDING OF ARCOM

In April 2005, I and some Congolese friends began drafting ARCOM's statutes. I then went to the G5 district to meet with Béatrice, a migrant woman of about fifty whom I had gotten to know when we were both in Casablanca trying, unsuccessfully, to register as asylum seekers. I told her about my idea of starting an association, and read her the draft of the statutes. She thought it was an excellent initiative, especially, she said, in view of the terrible situation of expatriates in Morocco. We decided to meet again soon and keep working on these plans to found an association. While I was in G5, I visited Sylvain and his wife, Michaux, told them what I was intending to do, and asked them to help spread the word. At church on Sunday I met with my friend Maman Astrid; she had also fled the DRC and lived in the same part of town as I did. I told her, too, about our plans, and asked her to invite other interested parties. I visited the Congolese migrants' prayer circles and invited people to come along. In this way, news of ARCOM's foundation was passed around.

About fifteen people turned up to the first meeting. It was really happening: we were united in working toward a common goal! I was delighted. However, I was also conscious that I had to be careful at this meeting. It was not possible to have the kind of discussion we used to have during my political life in the DRC. The majority of participants at this meeting were very skeptical about political activity. I knew it would be advisable to found an organization that pursued no party-political interests and was not profit oriented. Instead, its core mission should be to defend our rights and freedoms. I was the initiator of the organization, but all decisions should be taken democratically. We agreed that we would raise our hands to determine who was to speak. Everyone was free to propose people for election.

We began with the post of president. After five minutes of silence, broken only by the quiet whispering of those present, I raised my hand. After another moment of silence, one of those present spoke up. Turning to me, he said: "You are the initiator of this association, so to begin with you should lead it." When we eventually put it to the vote, everyone voted for me and applauded. One of the attendees invited me to stand and offer everyone juice. With this, the responsibility for our association was conferred upon me. At that moment, I felt that I was filled with tremendous strength. I was also aware that the task ahead of me was indeed a very weighty one.

We continued with the elections, deciding ARCOM's entire personnel structure. In addition to the president, we also elected two vice presidents, a secretary, a treasurer, and several advisers.

6

RAISING OUR VOICES, FIGHTING FOR OUR RIGHTS

As the leader of our association, I had to show commitment and creativity. My organizational skills were called for, too: I wanted to convince refugees and asylum seekers to stand up and fight for their rights. I would have to launch successful campaigns that would directly benefit members of the community. My job was to look after people in need; I had to be ready to listen to members, to support them and boost their confidence. Fortunately, I didn't have to do this alone. We formed teams that were tasked with listening to the worries and needs of our members. Astrid and Albertine, one of the other women who was present at the meeting and had been elected to a leadership position, took care of the women; I was there for the men. After meeting with a lot of different people from the community and listening to their concerns, it became clear to us that the problems they had, and the demands that were therefore being made of us, far exceeded our capacity for dealing with them. Most migrants lived in utter destitution. What were we to do? We ourselves had no means for conducting our political work, so the only possible way of finding a solution was to try to establish contact with Moroccan human rights organizations, and with churches, international organizations, and charitable groups. We were also on the lookout for individuals who might be able to help members of our community. I urged all members of our association to make everyone aware of any useful contacts, and to try to maintain good connections with any such people.

| MY CONTACTS

Before establishing ARCOM, I wanted to contact a number of local and international NGOs, as well as various political parties.

The first precautions I had to take concerned my appearance. I got myself a suit, a tie, and a good pair of shoes, so as not to evoke the negative image people have of migrants—and to keep from being stopped by the police or turned away by office doormen.

I had asked my contacts to put me in touch with people in positions of responsibility at a number of political parties and organizations. I visited the office of the UNHCR, where I was able to speak to Madame Fatima, the person responsible at that time for the protection of refugees and migrants. I was received there not as a refugee, but as the future spokesman of an organization that aimed to improve the situation of refugees and asylum seekers.

I was also received by senior members of several political parties, and was able to have a number of productive discussions. I particularly recall the conversation with the adviser to the head of a Moroccan political party. We had a long conversation about the current political situation in the DRC, and about the various parties in Morocco. He knew the DRC well, and told me many interesting things about the period when Lumumba came to power. As I was leaving, he said, "This is the first time I've had a political discussion with a young sub-Saharan African. Don't forget: Lumumba was about your age when he went into politics. I know that it's hard for the DRC to live in peace; it's because the country has such an abundance of natural resources. I'm glad young people like you are taking an interest in politics."

Another conversation I will never forget was the one with Saadeddine el Othmani, the current Moroccan prime minister, who at that time was the secretary-general of the Justice and Development Party, the JDP. It was a great pleasure for me to be able to meet the head of this important opposition party. Some people regard the JDP as an Islamist party, but it sees itself as a party that, while based on Islam, is primarily focused on fighting for justice and development in Morocco. We had a very long conversation, and I found him extremely attentive and likable. He took a keen interest in the situation of my country. I told him about the latest developments in the DRC, as well as about my former activities with the local UDPS youth organization. He asked me questions about the future of my country, following the outcome of the recent negotiations in Sun City. He also wanted to know what I thought about the appointment of the new government, and what our party's position was on that. I gave him my assessment: that the exclusion of our party leader, Étienne Tshisekedi, from the current government meant that the majority of Congolese people were extremely dissatisfied, and that the Sun City peace agreement was in jeopardy. Finally, he asked a few questions about my residency status in Morocco, and about my current activities. He also wanted to hear my impressions of the Moroccan political landscape. The conversation took place in a relaxed and friendly atmosphere. At the end, he handed me his business card and invited me to stay in touch. He also encouraged me to contact the other Moroccan parties.

However, not all my political encounters were successful. One party actually turned me away—I was told they wouldn't speak to me until I had a residence permit. There were even a number of NGOs who shut the door in my face because I had no papers. These were the same organizations that would later boast at international meetings and conferences that they were fighting on behalf of refugees and migrants in Morocco.

Nonetheless, I learned a lot from the contacts I made at this time. I was able to extend my knowledge of Moroccan politics and society; and I learned, among other things, that in Moroccan officialdom there were three things you were not allowed to question: the king, the nation, and religion. I also now had a clearer picture of which parties and groups we could work with and which we could not. These connections to people in positions of responsibility in various parties and organizations would prove very useful in the fight I was to engage in by establishing ARCOM.

Finally, it was imperative for us to have a fixed location where we could share our ideas and exchange information.

The first idea I had on this front was to contact Pastor Yves Vors. He represented the congregation of a French church with a branch in Rabat. I asked him whether he might be able to make a prayer room available to our association, because, as I've already described, Christian refugees and migrants were forced to hold their church services in secret in the ghettos, not daring to venture outside. I therefore decided to try to establish a framework that would enable all the informal churches that had formed in the ghettos to hold a communal prayer service at least once a week. At the same time, it seemed to me, these gatherings would strengthen the spirit of solidarity and mutual support within the community. What we needed to do was to find a room big enough for a large number of people where we could congregate in safety.

We described our situation to Pastor Yves Vors, and tried to explain to him the very difficult circumstances in which we were meeting to pray. We requested that he put the main hall of his church at our disposal once a week so we could hold a service in our own language, according to our own culture. The pastor was very open to our request, and gave his consent. We agreed that from then on we would congregate every Thursday from 10:00 p.m. until 12:00 a.m.

| PASTOR DAVID BROWN

One Sunday, after the regular service at Pastor Yves's Christian church, Astrid met a woman who worked at the embassy of the Central African Republic. Astrid told her about our association, and the woman said she knew an American minister who was renowned for helping sub-Saharan refugees and migrants. She invited Astrid to put together a delegation from our association and come by the embassy so she could put us in touch with the minister. Astrid, Albertine, and I went to the embassy of the Central African Republic, where we were warmly received by our new acquaintance. She told us about Pastor David Brown's activities and gave us his contact details. A few days later, we managed to arrange a meeting with him.

David Brown received us in the Evangelical Church of Rabat.

He told us he regularly helped refugees and migrants living in Rabat by providing them with food and clothing. Sometimes, he said, he would even come to the rescue when people had been thrown out of their apartments. David Brown had founded an association called Comité d'Entraide Internationale. Week after week, as part of his work with this organization, he met with migrants in distress and provided them with material help. His wife, Julie, was a nurse, and she also worked for the organization, ensuring people received the medicine they needed. The minister was indeed very familiar with the situation of refugees and migrants in Morocco, and he knew how to help them. His achievements were truly remarkable. We told him about our activities, and mentioned that we were also planning on starting a school project for the children. Pastor Brown was very interested, and promised to stay in touch.

At the end of our conversation, the minister indicated that he was very glad to have met us. He added that we should let him know when we were ready to proceed with the school project.

When we met Pastor David Brown, we didn't know that this encounter would save lives. Just a week after our meeting, a young man of about twenty came to see me early one morning. He was having great difficulty breathing, he said. He'd heard of ARCOM and hoped it might be able to save him. "President Emmanuel," he said, "I haven't been able to sleep properly for a week now. Often I simply can't breathe, and it feels as if I'm about to die. Please help me—I can't afford the medicine I need." I called Pastor Brown, who referred the young man to one of his social workers. They got him the medicine he needed, and the young man was saved.

From then on, Pastor Brown helped us with almost every

case we consulted him about. We will never forget the services he rendered to migrants and refugees.

| ARCOM AND THE DEPORTATIONS IN FALL 2005

On Saturday, September 17, 2005, starting at four in the morning, we received a series of phone calls from migrants living in the districts of Hay Nahda 2 and Takkadoum. They were frantic; they told us the police were in the middle of a large-scale raid. We couldn't call the UNHCR, as the office wasn't staffed at that hour of the morning—besides, no one worked there on Saturdays. Once again, we were lucky; our own apartment had been spared. It obviously paid off that we were as discreet as possible; hardly anyone had noticed our presence in the house.

By 7:00 a.m., more than 250 migrants had fallen into the clutches of the police, including 90 asylum seekers and refugees who were registered with the UNHCR. All of these people were being detained outside the police station in the third district, Hay Nahda 1. Then we heard that all the people who had been picked up would be taken by bus to Oujda on the Algerian border. Two Congolese women—one was pregnant, the other had her twelve-year-old daughter with her—collapsed before they could be taken away, and an ambulance had to collect them instead. The pregnant woman was in the hospital for two months. Her child died at birth. She remains traumatized to this day.

Maman Anny, the woman with the twelve-year-old daughter, managed to escape from the hospital the day of the raid. She and her daughter made their way to our apartment and got there at about 11:00 p.m. When they arrived, Maman Anny told us about the nightmare she had just experienced. "I was rudely awoken at four o'clock in the morning—the police kicked down the door of our house. They asked us for our papers. I showed them the confirmation I'd been given by the UNHCR that showed I'd applied for asylum, but they weren't interested. They took all of us with them, the other women and children as well. I was only wearing a nightshirt. While we were at the police station, I passed out. I can't remember anything after that. I woke up in the hospital. They examined me there and gave me medicine, then they put me in a hospital room, and I ran away."

From then on, Maman Anny was often sick. In August 2006 she died of a brain hemorrhage, and her daughter was left on her own. It was absolutely tragic. The last time I saw her, she said to me: "Papa Emman, do you know yet what's happening with the school project? We need a permanent solution for this problem. I don't want my daughter to go another year without school." Three days later—it was a Sunday—Astrid called me from the hospital's intensive care unit and told me that Maman Anny was in a coma. I got to the hospital as fast as I could. Besides Astrid, some other members of our association were there, and so was Dr. Kalonji. An emergency operation was performed, and with Pastor Brown's help we managed to get hold of a series of medicines, but it was all in vain. Maman Anny died three days later. May her soul rest in peace!

Police raids and brutal arrests were the most frequent cause of suffering and death among migrant women at that time.

The events of September 17, 2005, took their course. At 5:00 p.m. I received the first call from Oujda. Our friends informed us that they were locked up in cells and were now waiting to be deported to the Moroccan-Algerian desert. I decided to call a crisis meeting of the ARCOM leadership for that evening. We gathered all the information we could, and prepared a list of those migrants who were UNHCR-recognized refugees, or whose asylum application process was still ongoing. After conferring, we decided to go to the UNHCR office early on Monday morning and insist that the asylum seekers and refugees be allowed to return to Rabat. We already knew that the UNHCR in Rabat had a policy of keeping quiet: there had been a similar raid earlier that year, in May, and the office had done nothing whatsoever to protect the victims. Not even those in possession of UNHCR papers were given any help. Consequently, members of our association were demanding more and more forcefully that we organize a public sit-in outside the UNHCR building to condemn the silence of those in positions of responsibility and force the institution to act in the interests of the people under their mandate.

I fully supported this move. It was a good opportunity to protest not only against the UNHCR, but also against the Moroccan police. The office of the High Commissioner for Refugees was on one of the main streets in Rabat. All the police establishment's high-level decision makers went past it, as did high-ranking politicians. I believed that this was the right venue for a campaign of a kind Morocco had never seen before. I planned to bring all refugees and asylum seekers together for a joint protest against our friends' deportation. This attack on our basic rights should not go unchallenged.

And so we set to work. We set up a committee to mobilize and increase awareness among sub-Saharan migrants. On Sunday, we assigned someone in our group to take a communiqué to the Evangelical and Catholic churches announcing our intentions. The paper was read out in the various Christian churches.

The churches were sympathetic to our cause, but they didn't want to stick their necks out any further because of their uncertain status in Morocco.

As well as mobilizing people via the churches, we passed on information by word of mouth. We also contacted a number of Moroccan human rights organizations, including AMDH (Association Marocaine des Droits Humains), and SOS Racisme.

We began our campaign on that Monday morning. We headed to the office of the UNHCR, carrying various banners and shouting slogans. One banner read: "ARCOM condemns the illegal and unjustified deportation of sub-Saharan refugees and asylum seekers." Another said: "No to discriminatory deportations: We demand the immediate and unconditional return of our friends to their place of residence—Rabat."

When we arrived outside the building, we met a group of English-speaking asylum seekers whom our propaganda campaign hadn't reached. They had come to register with the UNHCR. However, when they saw that we had come to protest, they ran away, afraid of getting arrested along with us if the police showed up.

Around forty sub-Saharan migrants responded to our call. An Algerian refugee also joined our protest. However, the majority of sans-papiers living in Rabat stayed away from the demonstration for fear they would be arrested and deported. We went on chanting, but no one from the UNHCR came out. It wasn't until over an hour later, when a Spanish journalist arrived and started interviewing us, that the bureau chief, Madame Fatima, appeared. She and all her colleagues came outside and looked around. Then she called me over and asked me to put together a delegation, saying she was prepared to receive us and listen to our demands.

That day, I was filled with admiration for and pride in the courage of my friends. They were utterly determined, and every one of them made a contribution. I was especially impressed to see people chanting our slogans while handing out flyers to the police officers sitting in their buses.

An hour after the head of the UNHCR office came out to us, a six-person delegation was finally admitted to the building. The discussion was to take place in the conference room. Madame Fatima and four of her colleagues were present. Our delegation consisted solely of members of ARCOM: Albertine, Astrid, Pastor Albert, and myself, plus Raoul and Jérémie.

After a brief round of introductions, Madame Fatima started to speak—but she was not very welcoming. "If you want to talk to us, first of all, give us the rolls of film from the camera you took photos with outside. You don't have permission to take photos in front of our building." We didn't respond; in any case, someone had already taken the camera home. Madame Fatima repeated her demand. Finally, someone from our delegation replied that we didn't know the photographer. Madame Fatima became increasingly dismissive and edgy. "Why did you come here to make your protest?" she continued. "Are you demonstrating against us, or against the Moroccan authorities? Don't you know that the government carries out raids every year around Ramadan?"

This really was too much. I could see that all the members of our delegation were seething with rage. Albertine was the first to react. "You think our protest here is pointless?" she said. "So the women and children who are suffering in Oujda right now, as we speak—are they worthless to you? What exactly is the function of the UNHCR? We fled to Morocco to escape appalling circumstances, and here you tell us that it's normal to carry out raids! Is that really how you intend to protect refugees?" Pastor Albert, who was just as enraged as Albertine, also tried to say something, but without success; Albertine was unstoppable: "So you don't think it's worth bothering to pay any attention to our protest?!"

Pastor Albert finally managed to speak: "If we're of no importance to you, why did you issue us with papers?"

It was obvious that the head of the UNHCR office hadn't realized who she was dealing with. She had no idea about all the terrible things refugees and migrants had to deal with on their journey. Nor did she know anything about the torments many of her clients had suffered in their home countries. At the start of the meeting, she had exuded the same contempt for sub-Saharan Africans that we were accustomed to from the Moroccan press. As far as she was concerned, we were people of no worth, no culture, and no education. Worse still, in her eyes we were like a plague of locusts. She hadn't expected us to stand up to her. Now she felt obliged to change her tone: "We're aware of Saturday morning's events, and were deeply shocked when we heard about them. Since this morning, we've been in contact with the Moroccan authorities to clarify the situation. Before we continue our conversation, I'd like to let your president, Emmanuel, speak. I'd like him to summarize the events for us, and explain exactly what happened."

First of all, I attempted to defuse the tense atmosphere. "We're here because people have been deported to the desert. They're being subjected to terrible suffering. It's up to us now to find an immediate and appropriate solution, so it's better if we start this meeting without tension." I also apologized for the harsh tone taken by our side, and suggested we try to get back to a good climate for discussion. This proposal was well received by all present. I began to describe the events of the previous days, and passed on the latest information I had received from Oujda. I then reiterated our outrage at the deportations. I stressed that these deportations were in contravention of the 1951 Geneva Refugee Convention as well as the African Union's Refugee Convention. Morocco had signed both of these agreements, and must now abide by the ban on deportations. Finally, I asked the people in charge at the UNHCR to put together a team to drive to Oujda as quickly as possible and bring the deported refugees back to Rabat. This team should be accompanied by a member of our association. Again, I emphasized that it was important to act fast; there were pregnant women, children, and babies among the refugees. I handed Madame Fatima a copy of our resolution, which listed all of our demands. Madame Fatima didn't speak French, and had to have the paper translated for her by one of her colleagues. She then prepared to answer us, but before saying anything substantial she turned to the secretary of our delegation, who was taking minutes of the meeting, and said, "Discussions that take place in the UNHCR office are confidential, and you do not have the right to take notes. Nothing we discuss here is to go outside this room."

Once again, I realized that the person we were dealing with was not treating us with respect. Inside I was fuming, but I tried to control my emotions. Pastor Albert had once said to me that the spokesman of a group doesn't have the right to get angry in public, because in doing so he loses his credibility. So I tried to continue the dialogue, and to insist our demands be met.

We didn't manage to get them to agree to send a team to Oujda. Madame Fatima told us that the UNHCR just wanted to hear our side of things, and that they would see to everything else themselves. With that, the discussion was deemed to be over.

Before we left, Madame Fatima made one more outrageous demand: she insisted that we hand over all the paper we had made notes on during the meeting. We acceded to this, but we only gave her the unimportant papers. In any case, we remembered all the most important information. When we got home, we made detailed minutes of the entire meeting.

During the discussion with the UNHCR officials, I had realized that the High Commissioner's representatives were in a very weak position. They had a difficult relationship with the Moroccan authorities, and they didn't have the power to put together a delegation of their own and send it to Oujda. It was wholly unrealistic to expect that they would fetch the deported refugees back to Rabat. The only thing we could still do was to contact nongovernmental organizations and ask them for their support. And so, after our protest at the UNHCR, I called Helena Maleno, who worked in Tangier with the Spanish chapter of the organization SOS Racisme. I asked her if she knew any aid organizations in Oujda that could bring the deportees water, food, and blankets. She promised to look into it and call me back—but she, too, eventually gave me a negative answer. Both the staff of Doctors Without Borders and a certain Father Joseph Lépine, who was with the Catholic church in Oujda, were on holiday; they couldn't be reached.

We had to think of something. Feverishly, we considered how we might bring at least the women, children, and babies back to Rabat. We had to save them from the worst. After making countless phone calls, quite by chance we came across a migrant who had been deported to Oujda and who told us he still had 2,000 dirhams [$206] on him. We asked him to use this money to buy train tickets for the women and children with UNHCR documents. They should return to Rabat, accompanied by two or three men. We promised him we would reimburse the money in Rabat.

But things were much more complicated than we had thought. The deportees were stuck in a woodland outside Oujda; they were terribly weak, and desperate. Jean-Baptiste, one of the deportees whom we had asked to put together a group to travel back to Rabat, called us a few hours later and explained the situation. "We're in a dreadful mess!" he said. "We can only buy tickets for twelve women and children; there's no money for any more! Everyone wants to get out of here! The conditions we're being kept in here are appalling; it's driving people crazy. We haven't had anything to eat or drink since we were deported!"

"Jean-Baptiste," I answered, "try to keep a clear head. Make a list, and make sure that women with small children are evacuated first." He agreed, and promised that this was what he would do. But the battle was far from won. Around midnight, Jean-Baptiste called me again and informed me that he and the whole group of travelers—five women, four children, and three men—had been arrested by the police at the Oujda train station. "They threw us into prison cells! They couldn't care less that we have asylum application papers issued by the UNHCR." The news turned my stomach. It was the middle of the night; there was nothing I could do. I was terribly worried, and couldn't sleep all night.

The next morning—four days after the raid—we decided to involve the UNHCR again. We called their office, explained the situation, and requested that their officials send a fax to the police station in Oujda, demanding that the prisoners be released and given free passage to travel to Rabat.

This time, the UNHCR agreed to our request. The fax was sent. Two days later, at 7:00 a.m. on Thursday, the group arrived back in Rabat. They were all utterly exhausted, and some were seriously ill. One woman had with her a three-month-old baby with such a bad cough that I was truly frightened for the infant. Other women were extremely traumatized by the things they had experienced in Oujda.

We had succeeded in evacuating one small group. But what would happen to the people we couldn't get out? We decided to launch a solidarity campaign. Every member of our association was asked to make a financial contribution to enable us to bring back as many people as possible. Everyone gave what they could, and Pastor Yves Vors also supported us. In this way we were able to pay for several other migrants to travel back. They arrived in Rabat one week later.

The events of September 2005 were terrible, but for the first time we had tested large-scale strategies for action against the deportations. Our association had proved that it had the capacity to react appropriately in situations like this. Although we were working, for the most part, without any outside support, we were determined to defend our rights, and it was this determination that gave us energy. We had learned to combine our forces and our ideas, and to demonstrate what we were capable of. Our persistence, and our successes, also showed us that we could do more. A UNHCR official actually praised our initiative. "I congratulate you on your fight," he said. "Our boss was so taken aback by your commitment that she didn't know where to start."

There were indeed serious tensions between the UNHCR and the Moroccan authorities. The latter refused to recognize the resolutions that came from the High Commissioner's office. You could say that the UNHCR in Morocco was tolerated, but not fully accepted.

The situation only changed a little in 2007, following a major campaign by a number of Moroccan and international NGOs. After the crisis of 2005, Madame Fatima was replaced by the Dutchman Johannes van der Klaauw, who managed to extract a new agreement from the Moroccan government concerning the rights of the UNHCR. However, it would be wrong to assume that there were no more illegal deportations. The Moroccan police continued to refuse to recognize documents issued by the UNHCR. Despite the public attention the issue had attracted in the interim, deportations to the Algerian desert continued.

The UNHCR was still stuck between a rock and a hard place. On the one hand, the institution was obliged to guarantee the protection of refugees in Morocco; on the other, it felt constrained to fulfill the European Union's political agenda. It has to be remembered that the EU countries are the most important financial backers of the UNHCR in Morocco. Thus the Office of the High Commissioner for Refugees suddenly became an accomplice in the isolation of Europe and externalization of EU border protection. Refugees and migrants were just a pawn in the game of divergent interests. For the parties and institutions involved, we were just political small change. Instead of being given the protection we so urgently needed, we became an economic dividend.

| OPERATION GOUROUGOU: WOMEN AND CHILDREN

Gourougou is a small mountain village on the Moroccan border with the Spanish enclave of Melilla. In September and October

2005, there was a situation that came to be referred to in migrant circles as "Gourougou: Women and Children." For a limited period of time, women who were pregnant or traveling with their children were able to cross from Gourougou onto Spanish territory. A large number of female migrants and asylum seekers who had been living in big Moroccan cities—Rabat, Casablanca, Oujda, Tangier—headed for Gourougou. Hundreds of women and children were able to enter Spain during this period. However, there were also cases of women who had crossed the border being deported back to Moroccan territory.

Michaux, Sylvain's wife, and Ivette, two UNHCR-recognized asylum seekers, were both active members of our association. They couldn't tolerate the excruciating life of exile in Morocco any longer, so they also decided to take their children and try their luck. They crossed the border at night and were already on European soil when they were deported back to Morocco a few hours later by the Guardia Civil. I visited Michaux when she finally made it back to Rabat, and she told me what had happened.

"We crossed the border at about ten at night. We thought it would be easy. How wrong we were. We walked from ten p.m. until four in the morning; we crawled up a hill, waded across a river. One false step and we would have drowned. It was bitterly cold, and we were starving. We'd spent three days in the woods near Gourougou before this, waiting for an opportunity to scale the border fences, and we hadn't eaten or drunk anything in those three days. Our two children got sick: my son had such trouble breathing I was afraid he was going to die.

"We followed the directions we'd been given before we left, and tried to reach the main reception center for refugees in Melilla, but we didn't make it. Suddenly we were surrounded by police from the Guardia Civil. They shone their torches in our faces and asked us where we'd come from. Our children were terribly afraid; they were breathing faster and faster. One of the gendarmes took pity on us and actually wanted to take us to the reception center, but suddenly two more migrants who'd dared to cross the border materialized in the dark. The police asked us if they were our husbands, and we said no. We really didn't know the two men, but our situation suddenly became much more complicated.

"The police officers contacted their superior and consulted with him in Spanish. After a while, one of them looked at our children again and shook his head. Then they ordered us into the police jeep. We thought we were saved—that they were going to take us to the reception center in Melilla. Far from it. They drove us back to the Moroccan border, said, 'Goodbye,' and simply dumped us there.

"After that we were picked up by the Moroccan police and put in a cell where a lot of other migrant men and women were already being held. The prisoners included pregnant women and a number of other children. We spent a week in this cell, and then we were deported to Oujda, where we fell into the hands of a criminal gang that held us captive in our ghetto. I was lucky—whenever anyone approached us, my son started screaming. But he was forced to see the violent acts those criminals inflicted on other women, and it's traumatized him so badly that, ever since we got back to Rabat, he flies into a panic if a man comes anywhere near him."

It really was as Michaux described: her nearly one-year-old son couldn't bear my presence that day, although he had known me before they crossed the border.

Ivette, who had taken her little daughter with her on this

journey, told me later why the crossing had gone wrong. "The intermediary who was supposed to smuggle us to Melilla sent two men over the border immediately after us, who suddenly appeared out of the darkness like ghosts," she said. "The Guardia Civil policemen were on the point of taking us to the reception center in Melilla. The intermediary tricked us: he knew perfectly well that women are sent back if they're caught crossing the border with men." She was dreadfully depressed. "Papa Emman, just leave it," she said. "We experienced terrible things. I don't have any strength left. I doubt I'll ever have the courage to talk about what happened to us."

Béatrice, our colleague from ARCOM, had also tried her luck; she, too, had failed. After she set off, we didn't hear from her for two weeks. Normally, our friends always called us as soon as they got to the reception center in Melilla or Ceuta. At last the phone rang. "Béatrice, where are you?" I asked.

"Oh, Papa Emman—I was deported to Algeria." From her tone of voice, I could tell that she had endured torments. "We were arrested in Gourougou and brought to Oujda, where we fell into the hands of a criminal gang. They abducted us and took us to Maghnia in Algeria. They've let us go again, but I can't get back to Rabat now. I'm going to try to make my way to Algiers. Goodbye!"

Basically, the migrants' situation in Morocco had not improved, although ARCOM did its best to mitigate things. More and more often, we tried to inform the Moroccan and international public about the human rights abuses that were going on. We managed to establish contact with Radio France International, and succeeded in getting the broadcaster to report regularly on police brutality and deportations in Morocco. We sent countless e-mails to human rights groups and charitable organizations; we compiled lists with the names and registration numbers of those who had been deported, and we kept the UNHCR regularly informed about the situation of refugees and migrants.

| THE FIRST ARCOM CONFERENCE

We were constantly receiving information about people, including women and children, being deported and dumped in the desert; some of them even died. This forced us to come up with more effective forms of action. We realized that we were in extreme danger, and that courageous men and women were needed to face up to this terrible situation.

We decided to organize a conference, at which we planned to bring together members of the various migrant communities to analyze the current situation, exchange information, and improve contact with deportees. In addition, we wanted to agree within a larger framework on how to get even better at informing the public about the intolerable conditions in Morocco. But where were we to organize the conference? What infrastructure could we access at this critical time?

I decided to revive the contacts I'd made some time earlier, when founding ARCOM, with the various political parties. One of them was receptive to my request, and asked me to make a written application, which I did. Success—two days later I received confirmation that they would put a room at our disposal for the conference.

Now we had to start advertising the conference and inviting representatives from the various communities. We sounded people out to see who could make what contribution to the debate, and formulated concrete proposals for the program.

Our preparations were in full swing—but meanwhile the situation in Morocco was coming to a head.

| THE INCIDENTS IN CEUTA AND MELILLA

As we were mobilizing for the conference, I received a call from the local representative of our organization in the woods of Bel Younech, near the border with Ceuta. He sounded extremely agitated, and had an urgent message to pass on. He said to me, in Lingala: "President, the situation here is very dangerous. We've been surrounded by police units for three days now. We can't leave the woods, not even to get food. The situation is absolutely critical. Tell anyone who's planning to come here to forget it. It's too dangerous!"

Just a few days later, the same friend called me again. His report this time was even more worrying than before. At first, all I could understand was that the camp in the woods had been demolished and a lot of people wounded or killed. Then we were disconnected—my friend's cell phone had run out of credit. I topped up my own credit as fast as possible and called him back. When I reached him, he said, "You wouldn't believe what's happened. A lot of us stormed the border fences in a big joint action, because we were increasingly in danger from the Moroccan police. We had to find a solution, so we launched a surprise attack to try to get to Melilla. The Moroccan police and the Guardia Civil came. The policemen fired at us from close range from their respective sides of the border fence. I saw people being hit by bullets and falling right before my eyes. We still don't know exactly how many are dead. Fortunately, I didn't get shot, but I was arrested, along with many others. We're in the hands of the police, and we have no idea what's going to happen to us now. We urgently need your help. Put fifty dirhams' credit on my cell phone, first of all, so we can stay in contact." I promised we would pull out all the stops in order to help him, and I took down the numbers of others who'd been arrested, too, so I could be sure of reaching someone in case of emergency.

Never in all my life will I forget the dramatic events of Ceuta and Melilla in October 2005. Far more people died in the mass storming of the border fences than was claimed in the Moroccan and Spanish press. Most newspapers reported that twelve "illegals" were killed. But even if it had only been twelve—do the police have the right to shoot people, using live ammunition, just because they don't have papers?

We were still in shock on October 7, the day before the conference, when another terrible piece of news came in. Refugees and migrants in Gourougou had also attempted to storm the border fences en masse. We heard from one of those involved that here, too, people had died. Many others were arrested and deported—not to Oujda this time, but to an unknown destination. I contacted Helena from SOS Racisme, who had already heard the news. I told her that our conference was scheduled to begin the next day, but it was also imperative that we respond to these events. We were both well aware of the seriousness of the situation. We agreed that we would ask a number of Spanish and other European NGOs to send a delegation into the desert to take food and blankets to the deportees and bring them to safety. Helena promised to inform me as soon as she and the delegation had arrived.

At 6:00 p.m. on October 8, 2005, just as we were preparing to start our conference, we received the call from Helena, who had reached the deportees. She was beside herself.

"Emmanuel, the situation here is catastrophic!" she said. "The police are perpetrating an absolute bloodbath! There are more than two thousand migrants here, men and women; many people have died, and others are missing! The police have just beaten up two migrants right in front of us—they were refusing to get onto the police bus. There are international TV journalists here; they saw it, too. You have to respond! Call your embassies and tell them they have to take action, urgently! We've really got to talk about all this at the conference, too."

At the end of the conversation, she added: "I tried to find Issa, the Congolese chairman from the Bel Younech woods, but I couldn't—he's disappeared! It's absolutely terrible!"

We went to the building where the conference was about to take place and told all our friends there what had happened. All of us were completely stunned, shocked, and demoralized. We tried collectively to gather our courage and comfort one another. Pastor Albert said a prayer, placing the conference in the hands of God. He also prayed for all the deportees in the desert. Afterward, we left the room in silence.

The conference began at 8:00 p.m. Professor Kabasele Yenga Yenga opened the proceedings: he thanked all those present for coming, outlined the framework of the conference, and introduced me. Before starting my speech, I passed on to all those present the information we'd received from Helena. I then asked everyone in the room to rise and join me in a minute's silence in memory of the victims of these recent events. I spoke of all those who had lost their lives on the border fences of Ceuta and Melilla, and of those who had been left to die in the desert. Then I began my speech.

I spoke for half an hour. In this short time, I felt myself becoming reinvigorated. The conference was immensely significant for me. I criticized the Moroccan government's stance on migration, and examined the role of the European Union in detail. I explained that Europe was financially supporting the Maghreb countries' closure of the borders, and added:

"Part of the reason why these arrests and deportations keep happening is that the EU is pushing Morocco in this direction. Europe has to understand that it must tackle the cause of the problem, not its effects! The migratory movements from African countries, which Europe today finds so regrettable, simply highlight a situation that has long been kept hidden. The root cause of migration lies in the exploitation of Africa's resources by multinational companies! It lies in the fact that the EU continues to assure so many of Africa's corrupt and despotic governments of its support! It also lies in the negative consequences of the World Bank's and International Monetary Fund's structural adjustment programs. And let us not forget the so-called partnership agreements Europe imposes on Africa, the sole purpose of which is to provide an official and legal framework for the exploitation of African resources."

After my lecture, Professor Kabasele took the floor again, adding, "Who knows—perhaps one day people will live better in our countries of origin, which are so looked down upon today, than they do right now in Europe."

I began to realize that, as well as Congolese migrants, there were others present, too: from Liberia, Côte d'Ivoire, Mali, and Cameroon. As each requested leave to speak, it was clear that they were all highly educated and had a variety of skills. This showed once again that, contrary to what is often claimed, migrants are not people without education, values, or culture. Many of the skills I observed in the attendees simply could not be applied in their countries of origin—the dictatorial regimes in charge there prevented their development. Everyone at the conference was looking for a country where peace and justice prevailed.

The discussion that followed my lecture was very stimulating and interesting. We touched on a great many topics, and even managed to establish communications strategies that would enable us to contact migrants being held in the barracks in Guelmim in southern Morocco.

After the conference, ARCOM got back to work. The incidences of human rights violations continued. One of the many cases we dealt with was that of Philippe and Mahai, two Congolese asylum seekers who were deported to the desert. Mahai was still a minor. Their call reached us a week after the end of the conference. Philippe told me on the phone what had happened to them.

"We were arrested in Rabat. After five days at the police station, we were deported—not to Oujda, but someplace we didn't know, in the middle of the desert. We had no way of orienting ourselves. We wandered about in the desert for three days until our feet were swollen. Finally we reached a village, where a policeman picked us up and took us to a hospital. The doctor there was nice, and when he found out we were Congolese, he called the Congolese embassy. They gave him your number, so we were able to contact you. But we don't know what to do now. The UNHCR issued us with papers, but when they deported us, the police simply ripped them up. We also came across two other asylum seekers here, both women. One of them has two children with her, and a little baby."

| A COURSE ON ASYLUM-RELATED ISSUES

The events in Ceuta and Melilla in the fall of 2005, during which at least twelve people were killed at close range and thousands of migrants were deported to the desert, prompted a fresh wave of mobilization in Moroccan and European civil society. As I have already stated, these events also resulted in the former head of the UNHCR office being dismissed and replaced by Johannes van der Klaauw. Things had begun to move.

Under the new boss, the UNHCR office also changed its strategy. It organized a training course for agents of civil society, in collaboration with the French aid organization Cimade and the Moroccan organization AFVIC. The aim was to teach members of Moroccan and European human rights organizations, as well as refugees and asylum seekers, about the international instruments for the protection of refugees. They would also learn methods for raising awareness in Moroccan society about issues of flight and migration.

Aziz, a Cameroonian man I'd met at our conference, put our names down.

The course lasted three weeks and was held in Bouznika, not far from Rabat. I set off on November 25. For me, it was a blessing to be able to leave Rabat for a few weeks. It wasn't just the training course I was looking forward to; I would also have a little while to recover from all the terrible events, the raids and deportations and everything else we'd been through in the previous weeks and months. These trials had left their mark. I was completely exhausted. I'd been working very hard and had been constantly on the move, gathering information about deportees to pass on to the UNHCR and strengthening our contacts with human rights groups. It's also important to bear in mind how much energy it takes for people to keep on encouraging and sustaining one another, over and over again. I considered it one of my principal tasks to support and give strength to the men and women who'd been deported to the desert, and this task had completely preoccupied me. The shock of recent events had been so great that many of the active members of our association were now also completely burned out. I will never forget what an important role our comrades Astrid and Albertine played in our activities. They were tireless in seeking information about the victims of deportations, and they comforted us when we were down.

The small town of Bouznika is about fifty kilometers from Rabat. Aziz and I arrived at around nine in the morning and were met by Hicham Rachidi, a founding member of the Moroccan organization GADEM (Groupe antiraciste de défense et d'accompagnement des étrangers et migrants). After we had dropped off our baggage we were greeted by Anne-Sophie Wender, the head of the French organization Cimade in Morocco. She introduced us to other participants who had traveled there from the north of the country. The atmosphere was very friendly, and there was a spirit of solidarity. Hicham and Anne-Sophie took us to the dining room, where we all breakfasted together.

The first unit of the course was moderated by Anne-Sophie. She handed out teaching materials and explained the course's aims. The next three weeks would primarily be about reinforcing our capacity for action. We would learn how best to help in individual cases, and would become more skilled at integrating agents of civil society in the fight for refugee and migrant rights. By the end of the course, we should be capable of taking action at Moroccan, European, and international levels. Furthermore, the training aimed to equip us to initiate public campaigns that would draw attention to the rights of refugees and migrants. We were taught about networking, and trained in how to effectively gather information relevant to our affairs.

I quickly realized that this course would enable me to fill in a lot of gaps in my knowledge. Since founding ARCOM, we had always, until then, lacked an understanding of the international agreements on protections for refugees. We had never allowed this to hold us back in our desire for action, but it undoubtedly made sense for us now to be integrated into a wider network and increase our knowledge of the available courses of action.

During the last week of the course, Astrid, too, was invited to talk about her story, and to give an account of the life of refugees in Morocco. I would like to reproduce her speech here:

"I left my homeland, the Democratic Republic of the Congo,

in September 2000. In the time I have been on the road, I have witnessed countless acts of violence against women. I, too, have been a victim of violence. Today, I am actively involved in supporting and training women and children who have migrated to Morocco.

"I would like to tell you about the conditions on my journey, and about our lives in exile. In the majority of cases, women and children fleeing the DRC do so on foot. They cross entire regions, negotiate major rivers, and often have great difficulty accessing potable water and food. God's protection is their only hope. On their journey, many women become the victims of rape. They are forced to prostitute themselves, which exposes them to a high risk of infection. The strain of the journey means their children are also liable to fall ill. The weakest among them die. Lack of health care is a major problem. Unwanted pregnancies are common. Abortions are performed in inhumane conditions, and it's not unusual for women to die as a result.

"In my case, I fled my country after spending nine years in jail. I was imprisoned because of my husband's public role. I do not wish to speak here of the things I experienced in prison. Every day of my life they come back to me, like a never-ending nightmare. After my release I was able to escape from Kinshasa to Brazzaville, but I didn't even know the whereabouts of my parents and family, my brothers and sisters. When I reached Cameroon, I heard from a Congolese man whom I met there that my husband had been shot. My journey took me across many countries: from Cameroon I traveled on to Chad, then to Libya, Algeria, and finally Morocco. I have terrible memories of crossing the Sahara. But I was forced to cross the desert in my search for a place where I would be protected and respected. I wanted to start a completely new life; and, of course, I also wanted to find my loved ones again.

"On my journey I saw people die of thirst under the blazing sun. To this day, I, too, have wounds on my skin that were caused by the sun. Often we would walk in scorching heat. We frequently lost our way in the desert. Terrible things were done to the women; many of them were raped.

"After four years, I finally arrived in Morocco in December 2004. Here, I met other Congolese men and women. Together we decided to organize, and fight for our rights.

"I would now like to tell you about the conditions I live in here in exile. The atrocities we were forced to endure on our journey only got worse here in Morocco. Many women are forced to prostitute themselves, are raped, or are infected with diseases. Many migrant women also suffer from hunger; they are the victims of arbitrary arrests, and of deportations to the desert.

"It's almost impossible for refugees and migrants to integrate in Morocco. I'm a trained nurse, but I can't practice my profession because I don't have papers.

"I am convinced that the Earth belongs to all people, and that there should be no borders. I know that I have the right to seek a country that will give me asylum. With God's help, I will also find my family again; one day we will be reunited and will sit at the same table, eating and laughing.

"Among us refugees and migrants, there are academics and other well-educated people who are at their wits' end because they're denied access to the employment market. There are no jobs for 'azzis,' as we're disparagingly called. As well as acts of violence committed against refugees and migrants, there's also another problem that must not be swept under the carpet. Many

African countries refuse to recognize refugees on their territory. Furthermore, there are almost no UNHCR structures along the route from Cameroon to Algeria by way of Chad and Libya. There may be a branch of the High Commissioner's office in Cameroon, but it is closed and inactive, so many refugees find themselves in an extremely precarious situation. Even dogs have the right to life, yet this right is denied to refugees.

"It's also very hard for refugees to find suitable accommodation. The overcrowding of apartments leads to serious difficulties. People are attacked, forced into prostitution, and the lack of hygiene causes many health problems.

"In the majority of cases, the children of refugees and migrants are not accepted at Moroccan public schools. Trying to enroll these children is therefore a big problem. This is a key aspect of our fight. We are pursuing the objective of setting up a teaching center for migrant children so they receive a basic minimum of education. In spite of all our efforts and commitment, we have encountered great difficulties in implementing our plan. We don't have the funds needed to rent a schoolroom and purchase teaching materials. Nor do we have enough money to pay the teachers we recruit from our own ranks.

"Like many others, I cannot return to my homeland, as I would have to live in hiding and would be in constant danger of re-arrest. We call on the UNHCR in Morocco and on the international community to find a country that's prepared to take us. We have the right to life. I say this as a representative of all female refugees, asylum seekers, and migrants living here in Morocco. Thank you all."

Everyone in the room was moved by Astrid's speech. Some Moroccan women sitting in on our meeting were unable to hold back their tears. We interrupted the proceedings for a few minutes to give the participants a chance to digest what had been said.

As the three weeks drew to a close, we decided to establish an unofficial network and set up a mailing list, which we would use in the future to exchange all important information. I was very satisfied with the outcome of the course. It was particularly important that I had met these other activists. This network would make my work much easier in the future.

| SETTING UP A SCHOOL

As I explained in chapter 4, and as Astrid emphasized in her speech, the children of refugees and migrants in Morocco do not have access to education. Given this unacceptable state of affairs, we were firmly resolved to set up an education center—not just to provide schooling, but also to bring migrant children out of obscurity and, in doing so, achieve their integration into the official Moroccan school system.

Before we started to set up the center, Pastor David Brown recommended that we do the rounds of various schools in Rabat and try to register the children there. I went to lots of schools and spoke to the principals. Every single one informed me that they didn't have the right to enroll migrant children. The principals were under a lot of pressure, as this was not long after the events in Ceuta and Melilla, and the whole situation had become very tense.

When I told Pastor Brown that my tour had yielded no results, he said, "I'm not surprised the school authorities have rejected all our demands. I wanted to set up a similar project myself, and wasn't able to push it through. It now seems that setting up an autonomous center really is the best way forward. I support your idea with all my heart, but you will have to raise the bigger part of the money needed. Our church doesn't have the wherewithal for such a huge project."

I went home and told the people in our office about my conversation with Pastor Brown. They were discouraged to hear that he couldn't help us financially at that time, and advised me to abandon the project. However, it seemed impossible to me that we should simply abandon our plan. I wanted to keep going, to fight for our idea to be implemented.

But the three-week training course in Bouznika brought fresh impetus for our school project. Toward the end of our time there, Hicham Rachidi and Anne-Sophie Wender informed us that one of the trainers had donated 2,000 dirhams [$206], to be shared between two migrant organizations. When I got back to Rabat, I called a meeting so we could decide how to spend our half. Some women wanted to use it to buy sugar, soap, and other hygiene items, to be distributed to pregnant women. Others supported the idea of the education center. We set the money aside until we reached a unanimous decision.

The school project meant a lot to me, and I was constantly thinking about how we might implement it. One day, as I was walking around our district, I came across a building that clearly housed some kind of education center. I went up to the first floor and met the director of the center. He had rented four rooms in the house, in which classes took place. We got to talking, and I asked him whether he would be able to sublet two of the four rooms to us for three half-days a week. I also explained our difficult situation to him. The principal, who was Moroccan, was very receptive and friendly. He completely understood our concerns, as he himself had lived as a migrant in France. He agreed to rent us the rooms, and we settled on a rate. It was affordable, especially as the rooms were already furnished with everything we would need for teaching: desks, tables and blackboard were all already in place. I called another meeting, and reported on this new possibility for implementing our school project. Everyone agreed to the plan. Albertine started talking to people who might be able to teach the classes. A Congolese man called Martin got in touch, as did Elvis, a refugee from Brazzaville. Both were prepared to give lessons for free. I was pleased and proud that we would finally be able to get our project off the ground.

I went back to Pastor Brown in excellent spirits and reported on our progress. He congratulated us on our success. Now that we were able to put up a certain amount of our own money, he agreed to support the school project. He gave me money for teaching materials, and promised that the church would pay half the rent. That same evening we went around the whole district, inviting all refugees and migrants with school-aged children to come to the new ARCOM center the following Monday. The parents and children were delighted. One couple said to me, "Realizing this school project was an excellent idea. See for yourself—we live here with the children in this little room, day in, day out, from morning until night. They pick up everything the grown-ups do and say. That's very bad for their upbringing. We can scarcely breathe here!"

On Monday, January 2, 2006, our dream finally came true. I got up very early and went to all the ghettos to collect the children and bring them to the school.

After we opened our education center, I came to understand the suffering of refugee children even better. Many of them had stories that made you weep.

I remember one boy from Guinea who was about five years old. Astrid told me that he was mute, and his mother was very worried about him. I went to the tiny apartment where they lived, and told the mother about our school. At first she was very skeptical, and didn't want to send her son. I tried to convince her, telling her that her son's mutism might be connected to his isolation. After a long discussion, the mother agreed, and I picked the little boy up every morning, as I did the other children. Lo and behold, within just two weeks an immensely gratifying change had taken place: the boy wasn't just speaking, he'd become an even bigger chatterbox than all the rest! I could hardly believe it. The boy's mother was over the moon.

Another child I remember very clearly was a sixteen-year-old boy from Côte d'Ivoire who couldn't read or write. I met him outside the office of the UNHCR and invited him to come to our education center, and he agreed. After attending lessons regularly for a while, he asked me if I could give him individual coaching as well. A few months later he was able to read and write.

I also remember two little girls, ages six and eight. It was only with great difficulty that I managed to make it possible for them to come to school. They both lived with a woman of about fifty, who forbade them even to play with other children. The girls and their foster mother lived in the same apartment as one of my friends. Every time I visited, the two children would gaze at me sadly. It was obvious how much they longed to go to school. On one of my visits, I brought two bags full of school books and learning materials and gave them all to the two girls. It was a way of presenting the foster mother with a fait accompli. Finally, reluctantly, she agreed, and these children also started coming regularly to our school.

That first school year posed a lot of big challenges for us. We always had great difficulty finding the money for the rent, and it was only with considerable effort that we managed to keep things going. Thank God we succeeded in getting through the year. We wiped the sweat from our brows; it was as if we'd won a bet.

It was only at the end of the second year that our school operation was put on a solid footing. We managed to obtain an agreement with the UNHCR, which stipulated that the High Commissioner's office would cover the rent and pay for our teaching materials. Johannes van der Klaauw visited our education center with two of his colleagues and congratulated us on our work. Later, we even managed to convince the UNHCR to rent a house where the students could live. Astrid campaigned forcefully for this project. Five underage migrant girls, two of whom already had children, were able to move into this house. Little by little, we were able to provide more and more refugees and migrants with somewhere to live, regular meals, and education.

Pastor David Brown also remained a staunch supporter, continuing to help us with various things we needed for the running of the school. Once, he visited the school with his wife and daughter, and brought a big stack of teaching materials with him.

Over time, more and more organizations visited our education center, as well as activists and researchers from a number of

European countries. Heidi Mosimann from Bern, whom I met at a colloquium in Rabat, sent clothes and shoes from Switzerland for the children. Mehdi Alaoui paid the rent for a month after visiting the education center. A trainee from France offered to teach our children for a while for free; she was very touched by our initiative. And I will never forget the support we received from four Italian students: Martina, Claudia, Francesca, and Gianluca. After visiting our school, they sent us what was, by our standards, a significant sum of money. A Dutch researcher who visited us in the ghetto, Hein de Haas, also supported us financially after he returned home.

| THE MIGRANTS' MUSIC FESTIVAL AND THE ANTI-AIDS CAMPAIGN

When we founded ARCOM, our most important objective was to increase the visibility of refugees and migrants in Morocco and promote their many and varied talents. One day I had the idea of organizing a music festival as a contribution to the fight against sexually transmitted diseases. At the time, I was sharing my room with two musicians, Raoul and José. They were wonderful artists who played religious songs. However, in Morocco—a Muslim country—there was nowhere to perform their music. They had already recorded several albums, and hoped to find asylum in a country where they could sell their music successfully.

As well as helping to fight against AIDS, my aim was also for the concert to bring together refugees and sub-Saharan students. Mistrust of and antipathy toward refugees was very strong among some of the foreign students. They regarded us as "illegals," and even in the Catholic and Protestant churches, where we would congregate, there was an unbridgeable divide. It would never have occurred to the students, who were generally the children of rich, privileged people in their home countries, to include refugees from their own countries in their activities. In their eyes, we were uneducated and incapable of getting anything done. Students whose parents held high political office at home were particularly arrogant in their behavior toward us. They called us clandestins, and claimed that, by migrating, we had brought disgrace upon our country. Conversely, many refugees took the view that the children of the rich were only ashamed of our presence in Morocco because it highlighted just how badly their parents were running our countries. In spite of all these resentments, I wanted to bridge the divide, and invited a student choir to perform at the concert. They accepted my invitation.

After three months of preparation, during which we received financial and logistical support from various human rights organizations and Christian churches, we were able to hold the festival—the very first of its kind in Morocco. The Evangelical Protestant Church of Rabat served as the official venue.

The concert was scheduled to take place on a Sunday. By 3:00 p.m., the room was full. A large number of organizations sent representatives, including Doctors Without Borders, Médecins du Monde, the UNDP (United Nations Development Programme), Caritas, the UNHCR, and various Moroccan human rights organizations, as well as organizations of students and asylum seekers.

Everyone wanted to hear the migrants sing. The concert was a great success.

The students sang as well. Most of them were delighted at the way ARCOM had managed to stage such an event. My strategy worked: after this, there was greater trust between us and the students, and some ARCOM musicians even started singing regularly with the student choir.

Only one thing cast a shadow over the festivities. During her address, the president of Morocco's Association for the Fight Against AIDS claimed that migrant men and women were primarily to blame for spreading the disease in Morocco. She said that the regions with the highest rates of AIDS were also those with the highest quota of migrants.

| THE CONFERENCE AT THE INTERNATIONAL UNIVERSITY OF RABAT

In any case, the relationship between refugees and migrants on the one hand and the students on the other was significantly better after the concert. So it came about that the president of the Congolese student body invited me to give a speech at a gala event marking the DRC's Independence Day. Every year, the association of Congolese students and interns in Morocco organized a range of cultural activities on the anniversary of Congolese independence. He also gave me a number of invitations to distribute to other Congolese refugees and migrants.

On the day of the event, I set off for the university with a group of my compatriots. On the way there, one of them said to me, "Today is the day we're going to tell the students to stop calling us 'illegals.' They need to know that they're not worth more than us, even if they did travel to Morocco legally. We must show them that there are those among us who graduated from university back home, in much more difficult circumstances than they have here in Rabat!"

That day, on the university campus, it was impossible to differentiate between students and refugees. Everyone was very dressed up.

A man of about sixty was there. He had studied in Switzerland and France; then, in the 1980s, he had returned to the DRC to put his knowledge at the service of his country, and had fallen afoul of the Mobutu regime. He told us that he hadn't wanted to get tangled up in the corrupt practices so typical of the country's leadership at the time. He preferred to remain poor and without influence. When the situation in the DRC failed to improve after the change of government, he joined the protest movement, and eventually had to flee. Now he, like us, was stuck in Morocco. We dubbed him "Ambassador of the Democratic Republic of the Congo in Morocco," and flocked around him to pay our respects.

At the entrance to the university buildings they almost didn't let us in. The doormen couldn't tell that we weren't students, but they still asked to see ID. It was only when one of the conference organizers, who was at the university, hurried over that they opened the door for us.

Altogether, four people were to speak: a doctor who used to work for the Mobutu family, a journalist, the secretary of the Congolese embassy, and me. My speech was entitled "Changing the Political Order in the DRC as the Only Effective Measure in the Fight Against Enforced Migration." As you can imagine, it caused great displeasure among the diplomatic corps, as well as with the old Mobutists. I didn't mince my words when listing the reasons for our migration; I talked about the human rights abuses taking place in the DRC, the poverty and underdevelopment, and pointed out that the roots of these injustices were the dictatorship, and bad governance. After this analysis of the current situation, I declared that there had to be democratic change in the DRC. Without a functioning constitutional state and a fair economic order, I argued, there could be no development in Africa. I drew attention to the huge discrepancy between the riches of the continent and the poverty of its people.

"It is obvious, then, that our governments are not doing their work well! Look at all the development aid the DRC has already received . . . and yet no development happens. The governments of the last few decades thought they were not accountable to the people. They robbed the country of its riches, built palaces for themselves and their families, and transferred the stolen money into foreign bank accounts. They thought—and still think—they could act outside the law. All those who dare to raise their voices against them are silenced. They are murdered, or thrown in prison. In these circumstances, how can we speak of development in Africa? How can it be possible to move the continent forward with governments like these?

"In my view, the first step toward change must be to make it possible for the people freely to elect a government. It must also be possible for the people to check up on this government, and, if necessary, to vote it out. Only in this way can the country be administered to the benefit of the population. Only in this way can there be sustainable development."

I ended my speech with the laconic observation that the Congolese diaspora would only be able to take an active part in the development of Africa after the establishment of a new political order.

My speech was positively received by many of those present. Some started shouting: "UDPS, UDPS!" It was a major blow for the diplomats in the room, and for the secretary of the Congolese embassy, who was sitting beside me. He found it very difficult to present his conference paper after my speech.

After the speeches, there were questions from the audience. A student who had traveled in from Oujda confirmed our opinion about resentment toward refugees within the student community.

"You illegals," he said, "what are you actually doing here in Morocco? So many of you come to Oujda, from Algeria, too. I see how you suffer in winter." He turned to me. "You say you're their president. So what are we supposed to do with all the illegals arriving in Oujda?"

I answered, "The people you call 'illegals' are your fellow countrymen and -women. Many of them went to university, like you. Perhaps you will only realize after you've finished your studies why those you call 'illegals' have come to Morocco. Also, you shouldn't forget that you don't necessarily have to come via the Sahara to be illegalized! The same thing can happen to foreign students. In many cases, the Moroccan authorities refuse to extend their residence permits after they graduate. I'm sure there are some here among our student friends who've also been affected. Given the dreadful situation in their home countries, they, too, would rather attempt the crossing to Europe, or stay in Morocco without papers. So what do you suggest—what label should we give them? Aren't they 'illegals,' too?" You could have heard a pin drop when I finished speaking.

| THE REFUGEES' PROTEST OUTSIDE
THE UNHCR OFFICE

Despite our activities, our situation in Morocco remained very difficult. Sub-Saharan African refugees and asylum seekers were no longer prepared to tolerate the miserable conditions in which they were forced to live. There was also increasing resentment toward the Moroccan state. It was completely absurd that authorities were still maintaining their policy of categorically rejecting refugees and migrants. Those affected turned to our association and the organizations of other communities, demanding that we put even more pressure on the UNHCR so a solution would finally be found. Many asked me to represent them at the High Commissioner's office.

A woman living in Morocco with her two daughters said to me one day, sobbing: "Papa Emmanuel, you are our representative, you have to do something for us. I can't stand it here any longer. Perhaps you can bear the pressure; you're alone here, and you're still young. But we women suffer things you simply can't imagine. The situation here is almost impossible for me and my two daughters to bear anymore. It breaks my heart to see my daughters being abused here. If it carries on like this, one of these days I'll die of worrying about them. If you don't do anything for us, we'll take our fate into our own hands," she continued. "Our situation is becoming increasingly unsustainable. You have to go to the UNHCR and demand a permanent solution for us!"

She said all this without asking me what I myself had endured. My situation wasn't that great, either—I hadn't seen my family in years, and the news reaching me from the DRC meant all hope of a positive development was vanishing.

However, this woman was serious about making these demands of me. She went to Astrid and complained to her as well; then an hour later she came back to my house, this time with a whole group of refugee women. One of these women held up a kilo of semolina and shouted at me: "President, you're an adult—you can't claim you knew nothing about it! You're very well aware of the way things work here! Last night I had to sleep with a stranger so I could buy this bag of semolina for my little daughter! We've had enough!"

The women made such a noise that it attracted the attention of the landlord, who came to the door with his wife and threatened to evict me if my visitors didn't leave right away. The women promised him they would go, but after he left, one of them said to me: "Fine—we'll give the president, his deputy, and the office a little time to confer. If nothing happens, we can come back tomorrow and make a racket again. Perhaps our Mr. President will find it easier to get moving if he's evicted."

The women had put me in an extremely difficult situation. I was very worried, and immediately phoned the other members of the office to call an extraordinary meeting. We decided to confront the UNHCR again.

We got an appointment for July 20, when we took a delegation to the office of the High Commissioner. There we detailed yet again the urgency of our request. We made clear that our living conditions were worsening by the day, and that ten asylum seekers and a recognized refugee had died violent deaths in the months of May and June 2007. Finally, we renewed our demand that the UNHCR take immediate action to find a permanent solution for us.

The UNHCR staff replied that they would try to provide us with microcredits to promote our financial independence and make it easier for us to integrate into Moroccan society. We returned to the ghetto to report back to our people. It was already late in the evening, but a large crowd of refugees and migrants were waiting to hear what we had achieved. This time, though, my report did not get as favorable a reception as on previous occasions. When I said the word "microcredit," it was as if I'd rubbed salt in a wound. A furious woman cut me off: "President, if that's the solution you're offering, we withdraw our confidence in you! How can you talk about microcredits when we don't even have residence permits here in Morocco? Don't you know that the papers issued to us by the UNHCR aren't recognized by the Moroccan authorities? Every day our people are being arrested and deported to the desert. You've done nothing about it!"

Another woman continued: "Prepare yourself, President! We're going to hold another sit-in outside the UNHCR office, and we won't budge until they find a permanent solution for us! We demand to be granted asylum in a safe country!" Someone else stood up and said, "President, if the Moroccan authorities won't give us residence permits, and block our access to the job market and to social infrastructure, it makes no sense for us to fixate on staying in Morocco. You can't integrate people into a society where they aren't welcome."

The following day, I was visited by the representatives of two other refugee groups, one from Côte d'Ivoire and the other from Liberia. They suggested that we convene a meeting of all the spokespeople for the refugees and asylum seekers. We had to meet that very evening, they said. The situation was serious, and there was no time to lose.

The meeting took place in the apartment of a member of another refugee group and was attended by more than thirty people from several different countries. At the end of the session, we unanimously agreed to hold an open-ended sit-in outside the office of the UNHCR, with the sole aim of obtaining guaranteed asylum for all refugees and migrants in safe third countries, outside Morocco. During our debate, we reached the conclusion that it would be impossible for us to get the Moroccan authorities to accept our demands. Calling for integration into the regular job market or the legalization of our residency seemed unrealistic, and relocation to a safe third country the only practical demand we could make. We decided to launch our action on July 24. Each community was charged with mobilizing its members.

We met outside the UNHCR building at 8:00 a.m. on the agreed-upon day. Everyone had responded to the appeal launched by their respective organizations—men, women with children, boys, and girls—but they weren't there out of duty; they had all had enough. They were no longer prepared to accept that their human dignity should be trampled underfoot. Gradually, the journalists we had contacted also started to arrive. Our signs and banners bore the slogan: "UNHCR: We demand a solution!" At about 9:00 a.m., the office employees came outside, seemingly surprised to see such a large number of protesters. Around 11:00 a.m. the police arrived, as we were growing increasingly noisy, shouting and singing our slogans. The police chief asked us why we were there, and we explained the purpose of the sit-in. After a while he went over to a UNHCR employee and asked him to receive us. He hoped that this would bring the protest to an end.

At around 1:00 p.m., the UNHCR finally agreed to receive us. We put together a delegation that represented all the participating organizations and groups, and were led into the garden of the building, where we were received by the chief of mission,

Johannes van der Klaauw, his colleague Anne Triboulet, and Madame Asma, from a Moroccan organization associated with the UNHCR. After a short round of greetings and introductions, Ali, our delegation's spokesman, was invited to speak. Ali was the representative of the refugees and migrants from Côte d'Ivoire. I liked this young man a lot. When he spoke, he always got straight to the point, no beating about the bush.

Without further ado, he explained why we had initiated our sit-in. "We, the refugees and asylum seekers in Morocco, have had enough of our miserable situation," he said. "We've already suffered far too much. Because we don't have residence permits, we're not allowed to work, we have no money, and we can't pay our rent. Sick people are driven away from the hospitals. This inhumane situation in which we find ourselves has claimed the lives of ten asylum seekers in the past two months. The various discussions we've had with you lately have produced no results. Consequently, the members of our associations have lost faith in us. They don't feel we're doing a good job of representing them anymore. This is why the grassroots decided, of their own accord, to organize this sit-in. They all want a permanent solution, and we're aware that the only possible permanent solution is for us to leave Morocco and receive protection from a safe third country." He added that we were well aware that the UNHCR had to follow the political agenda prescribed by its main financial backer, the European Union. However, Ali continued, the UNHCR also had to acknowledge that the reality here in Morocco called for other solutions.

Johannes van der Klaauw started to respond. He spoke again about the microcredit project, and explained that the UNHCR had found a partner with whom this plan could now be implemented. As far as health care was concerned, van der Klaauw said we were still reliant on the Moroccan health-care system; the UNHCR simply didn't have the resources to run its own hospital. However, he added that he wanted to entrust the issue to a number of Moroccan health organizations and doctors, with a view to improving the health situation for refugees and migrants. Regarding our last and most urgent point, he said only: "Resettlement in other countries is just a possibility. You don't have any legal entitlement to it." And he added, "I'm asking you now to calm your people, and go home."

That was when I spoke. After our last meeting, I was very well aware of what our people thought and felt.

I started with a criticism of the microcredits. "In the Moroccan context, it's almost impossible for us to create an income using microcredits. We refugees and migrants are illegalized, and the papers you issue us with are worth nothing in the eyes of the Moroccan police. This is also the reason we live in constant fear of being arrested and deported. Besides: in order for a microcredit project to work, it's not just the financing that has to be arranged. There's also the question of marketing. If we manufacture products, or offer services, we also need to be in a position to sell them. Here in Morocco, no local is going to buy products from a sub-Saharan migrant, and we ourselves have no purchasing power. So how is this microcredit project supposed to work?"

I went on: "This is why we're demanding to be resettled. The legal situation here in Morocco has made us extremely vulnerable. We're condemned to inactivity, and we live in constant fear. We want to work, not to be forced to beg! I myself, for example, have made repeated attempts to find work at a call center. My qualifications met the requirements, but I was always rejected at the last minute because I didn't have papers! To this day it remains impossible to integrate refugees and migrants in Morocco. We are therefore calling for a permanent solution for everyone—and this solution can only consist in us leaving for a safe third country."

We refused to back down, and really read the UNHCR official the riot act. A woman from Côte d'Ivoire continued our indictment with reference to the situation for refugee women. "I am not ashamed to stand here in front of you and tell you that I was forced to prostitute myself in order to feed myself and my daughter," she said. "And yet I'm no longer young. I live in fear that my daughter will be forced to go into the same line of work in order to see us through. I appeal to your conscience and entreat you, as a matter of urgency, to find a country that will give us asylum. We would go to African countries, too, if only we could be safe there and have regularized status."

There was no solution in sight, so we interrupted the meeting and went out to the other protesters to report on the progress of the negotiations. Once we had passed on the information, it was unilaterally decided that we would continue the sit-in until a solution had been found.

Everything was fine until 6:00 p.m., at which point the police came and threatened to clear the square. One of our fellow campaigners suggested we seek shelter in St. Peter's Cathedral, just a few meters from the UNHCR office. I joined a reconnaissance party that was sent ahead to check out the situation at the church; the others would follow later.

We entered the cathedral by a side door, and called our intermediaries to let them know that the demonstrators could follow. Utterly exhausted, we lay down on the benches and floor of the cathedral to rest, at least for a while. We then contacted the priest in charge, Jean-Pierre, to inform him about the situation. I could immediately tell, when he arrived, how moved he was by what he saw. Our plight wasn't new to him, but he was surprised that we had gone so far as to take this step. A small group of us sat and talked to him in the meeting room of the church. We explained that we had come here from the UNHCR, because they hadn't offered us a solution, and because the police had threatened to clear the square. The priest called the bishop, who arrived shortly afterward. He, too, seemed sympathetic to our protest, and organized food and drink through Caritas. We hadn't eaten anything since the morning. The bishop also called the UNHCR, but we were not informed of what was said. Finally, he arranged for the security officials for the city of Rabat to come to the cathedral. When these municipal officials arrived, we called another meeting. It was decided that we could remain in the cathedral, and that a Caritas employee would be responsible for supplying us with food and drink.

Our relief was premature. We hadn't even finished eating when police officers forced their way into the cathedral. In the presence of the bishop, they ordered us to leave the church immediately. They said that in Morocco the Catholic churches also belonged to the Kingdom; we should not imagine we were in one of the churches of our homelands. If we wanted to protest, the police said, we should occupy the UNHCR. The High Commissioner's office was United Nations territory, whereas they had a duty to protect the church. Before we knew it, we had been thrown out of the cathedral and were standing outside the church doors. Voices were raised; many people would not accept this defeat.

And so the procession made its way back to the front of the UNHCR building, and we stayed there for another four days and nights.

Tensions rose as the days went by. Morocco was preparing to celebrate the anniversary of its independence. A lot of foreign guests were expected for the festivities. All public rallies and demonstrations had been prohibited. The police came back, and again ordered us to leave the square. We refused. Police officers kept coming and going. They spoke with the UNHCR and repeated their demand for negotiations. The officials in the High Commissioner's office agreed, but proposed that the discussion should take place somewhere else. We rejected the offer.

On the fourth day of our protest the police issued a final warning. We were ordered to leave the square immediately. The reason was obvious: the festivities were due to begin the following day. A refugee who was a former soldier told us in confidence: "The situation is deadly serious. We should break up the protest, otherwise people are going to die here. I was in the army, I know what it means when they issue a warning like that."

He was right. Within ten minutes, we were surrounded by heavily armed police officers. But no one seemed to want to give up. A lot of Moroccan and European human rights organizations were there, keeping track of the situation. In the midst of the chaos, a student I knew who worked with a refugee NGO came up to me and said, "Emmanuel, you're well regarded by the protestors. I beg you, be sensible—tell the people to go home. We have to make sure there's no bloodshed!" I decided to take the risk of addressing the protestors in order to get them to back down. But I had misjudged the situation. No one wanted to give up; the women, in particular, protested against my suggestion and refused to listen. "Emmanuel," one of them shouted, "if you're afraid of death, then go! I have nothing more to lose, I have no fear anymore!"

And so we stayed. I had already understood that, if things escalated, the UNHCR would deny all responsibility. We had to think of something else. Meanwhile, more police reinforcements were arriving, with other units coming to join them. At 4:00 p.m., the chief of police repeated his warning: "By seven o'clock this evening I don't want to see any of you here anymore!" The crowd protested noisily.

At 5:00 p.m., I got a call from Pastor Brown. He promised that he would be with us in half an hour, and told me he had also already spoken to Johannes van der Klaauw. When the pastor arrived, he summoned the leaders of all the refugee groups and told them, "The situation is very, very serious. Unless you do something right now, the police are going to crack down on you with utmost force. I'm very scared that people will die. Please, trust me—do everything in your power to end the protest here, so that we can all go to the Evangelical Church together as quickly as possible. You can stay there for the time being. Johannes van der Klaauw and the UN envoy here in Morocco will come to the Evangelical Church to discuss your demands. If they don't keep their promise and don't show up, you can come back here and continue your protest after the Independence Day celebrations."

When he had spoken, Pastor Brown asked me to relay this suggestion to the crowd. All the representatives of the different refugee communities rallied round me and endorsed the pastor's plea. I addressed the protestors. "My friends! If we weren't suffering so greatly in this country, none of us would ever have had the idea of holding out here for four whole days and nights. But look around you—we're surrounded by police, all of them armed to the teeth. All that's needed is a single word from their chief and they will attack. We mustn't give them the opportunity to shoot at us. Let's put our trust in Pastor Brown! You all know him; you're aware of his commitment and solidarity. Let's all go with him now to the Evangelical Church and stay there until a solution is found for us. The head of the UNHCR and the UN envoy here in Morocco will come and speak with us."

When I finished my brief address, the police chief came over. My words were welcome to him, of course, and he said cajolingly, "Yes, my friend, leave this area. You can come back here, to the UNHCR office, the week after the celebrations. We'll be receiving a lot of important guests, you see. You could stay here, but unfortunately there are many people among you who have bad intentions and are seeking to drag the reputation of the Kingdom through the mud. If a solution still isn't found for you after you come back here, Morocco will impose sanctions on the UNHCR."

At any rate, we had prevented the worst. The crowd headed to the Evangelical Church.

Then, shortly before midnight, Johannes van der Klaauw and the head of the United Nations office in Morocco came to see us at the church. We withdrew to one of the church's meeting rooms with them and Pastor Brown. Ali, our movement's spokesman, presented our demands again and tried to make the head of the UNHCR understand the seriousness of the situation.

We negotiated for four hours, until daybreak. Toward the end of the discussion, some of the refugees who had been delegated to the meeting began to fall asleep. But each party stuck to their positions: the UNHCR kept talking about microcredits,

while we insisted on resettlement in safe third countries. Pastor
Brown seemed very frustrated, and left the room.

On several occasions during our protest outside the UNHCR,
we had compiled a list of those who intended to stay overnight.
We knew, then, that on some nights 80 refugees and migrants
had camped out in front of the building. During the day, an estimated 150 to 200 people had taken part in the protest. Now,
though, on our first night in the Evangelical Church, our numbers increased dramatically. The news that we were occupying
the church had spread like wildfire, and suddenly more than
350 people had gathered there. Even refugees who didn't live in
Rabat had traveled to be there. The church was bursting at the
seams. At the same time, though, the talks with the UN representatives had failed. Pastor Brown could no longer guarantee
the safety of the people in the church, and was clearly starting
to feel afraid.

It was at this point that the UNHCR made a clever move.
The officials promised that the occupants of the church would
be received at the office the following Monday, and that each
and every one of them would be given a sum of money with
which to buy food and other essential items. The head of the UN
office in Morocco did the same, offering us a one-off payment.
Of course, this was far from being a real solution. But we were
all utterly exhausted, and Pastor Brown kept going on about how
he could no longer guarantee our security. He was terribly disappointed by the outcome of the negotiations. He, too, had run
out of ideas; the only thing he could think to do was to ask us all
to go home.

Naturally, we, too, were extremely disappointed. The women
in our movement, in particular, saw the end of the protest as a
major defeat. At the same time, though, it would be true to say

that the worst was averted. A year after I left Morocco to go to the Netherlands, a similar refugee protest came to a violent end. The movement had organized a sit-in outside the UNHCR, just as we had done. The refugees stayed there for a week. At that point, the police stepped in and a bloodbath ensued. Men and women were severely beaten; some people died of stab wounds. I was following the events from abroad, and saw photos of the police violence. It must have been horrific.

| MORE RAIDS AND DEPORTATIONS

During the night of December 23–24, 2006, at around five o'clock in the morning, I received a call from a member of our association. He was beside himself. He told me that yet another large-scale raid had just begun. UNHCR-registered refugees and asylum seekers were also being picked up. I had less than a minute of credit on my cell phone. I decided to call Johannes van der Klaauw. A familiar problem for a migrant in Morocco: your phone card has run out and you can't make the necessary calls, not even in the direst of situations. Luckily, van der Klaauw called me back when my credit ran out. He told me he was on his way to the airport and had to go abroad. However, he added that I should do all I could to find out the names of those affected who were covered by the UNHCR's mandate. I was to make a note of their ID numbers and give them to him. I could only do this, though, if I got new credit for my cell phone. The raids were well under way, but I had to go out nonetheless. Buying a phone card was too dangerous; I had to make calls from a public phone. It was a perilous situation. I risked being picked up and taken back to Oujda—but when I was elected president of ARCOM, I had promised to fight with all my power on behalf of refugees and migrants. So I slipped into my coat, pulled my cap right down over my face, and prepared to hurry out to the nearest call box. But before I could leave the house, Arthur and Ivette, two members of our association, came running up. Gasping for breath, they told me that more than fifty refugees had just been arrested in a building around the corner and were being taken to the police station. I quickly recounted my conversation with van der Klaauw, and all three of us ran to the call box. First, I called a woman who I knew had been arrested. She told me that all the sub-Saharan Africans in the building where she lived were now under arrest and being held at the police station. Two police buses full of migrants were already on their way to Oujda. She was in the middle of telling me the names of those affected when I suddenly saw three police buses turn the corner right in front of us. Our hearts leaped into our mouths. I dropped the receiver and we ran as fast as we could, racing through the streets, praying that we wouldn't fall into the hands of the police. After a few minutes we came to a mosque and hid behind it. We were just about to flee to the adjoining neighborhood, Hay Nahda 2, when a kind young Moroccan woman saved us by tipping us off. "Don't go to that neighborhood," she said, "the police are crawling all over it!" I had the idea that we should take the public bus to the medina quarter in the center of town and seek refuge in the UNHCR office. It was the best solution at that moment, but Ivette, who was terrified, said that her seven-year-old daughter was still at home and she couldn't possibly go without her. We told her to fetch her child, but knew that we would have to get out of there the minute a bus appeared. We couldn't wait for her out on the street. Sure enough, just moments after she left us to go back, a bus came around the corner and we leaped on. The passengers stared at us in astonishment.

At around 6:30 p.m. I got a call from one of the people who had been deported. He told me they ought now to be arriving in Oujda, but the police bus had taken an unusual route and was heading away from the town again. I was very afraid that they would be taken out into the Sahara, as people had been in October 2005 after the storming of the borders with Ceuta and Melilla. Half an hour later, the same migrant called me again. My fears were confirmed: the buses, six in all, had not stopped at the police station in Oujda, but had driven straight into the desert. They were obviously being taken to the border zone between Morocco and Algeria. Nor did the buses all stop in the same place; instead, they scattered their passengers in different areas, so that none of the groups knew where the others were. Apparently, it was also bitterly cold and raining.

What we found out later was appalling. Women and underage girls were raped; there were some brutal attacks. Some deportees actually lost their minds in that desert. One group was deported right into Algerian territory, where they were arrested by the Algerian police and robbed of all their possessions. In this group, too, people were raped, before finally being chased back onto Moroccan territory.

In October 2005, the Moroccan police had not been able to choose the timing of their operation. This time, though, they had deliberately timed their raid to coincide with Christmas. Their calculation was that there would be less resistance, as the NGOs and international institutions were on holiday. But the police strategists had grossly underestimated the dynamics of the refugees' and migrants' self-organization. Within a few hours, we had succeeded in spreading news of the raids and deportations all over the world. We alerted all the organizations and groups whose representatives were abroad. We sent reports about the course of events via the Internet. The information spread like wildfire, and we received declarations of support from all over. Johannes van der Klaauw cut short his holiday to return to Morocco. For the first time since taking office, he broke the UN's silence and condemned the deportations in a statement to the French press agency AFP.

A number of European organizations headed for Morocco, traveling to Oujda to bring the deportees blankets, warm clothing, and food. Meanwhile, we convened a crisis meeting of all the NGOs and human rights groups, which was attended by Doctors Without Borders, ATTAC Maroc, Médecins du Monde, Caritas, and two members of the European Parliament, among others. We established a number of commissions tasked with maintaining contact with the UNHCR, the Delegation of the European Union to Morocco, and the Moroccan Human Rights Council. Another commission was to exert pressure on the Moroccan interior ministry and demand that the deportees be allowed to return to Rabat.

I was on the commission that went to the office of the European Union. We were received by the spokesman for migration and asylum. I had long wanted to speak directly with the European Union's representatives and find out their position on the deportations. When we had explained why we were there, the spokesman had the audacity to ask why we had come to EU headquarters about this issue. We answered that we knew the EU was exerting pressure on Morocco to seal the borders with Europe. The official dodged our accusations and said he would contact the UNHCR and the Moroccan authorities to help us with our problem.

We, however, refused to be fobbed off. I spoke up, going even more on the offensive. "The EU needs to be aware of its responsibilities!" I said. "The men, women, and children who've come here didn't leave their countries just for the fun of it! The problem is that Africa's corrupt regimes are perpetually supported by Europe. Don't you think it's pretty remarkable that there are hardly any arms factories in our countries, yet wars on the African continent are constantly spreading? Why won't you admit that the real backdrop to these terrible conditions is the exploitation of our continent's natural resources! The solution cannot be that the EU gives Morocco money to close the borders, and simply accepts that refugees will be carted off into the desert and dumped there like sacks of rotten tomatoes."

I called on the EU representative to campaign for all the migrants to be returned to Rabat. I pointed out to him that it made no sense to decide between those whom the UNHCR had issued with papers and those who had been refused. "In these circumstances, it is discriminatory and, quite simply, inhumane to pit registered refugees against other migrants. What is happening here is a fundamental attack on human dignity, and it is our conviction that everyone is entitled to protection. The rich countries of the north have to finally stop forcing us into different pigeonholes. In segregating us like this, they are justifying racism in their own countries. All they're really trying to do is evade their international responsibility!"

It seemed, though, that we were not going to get anywhere

with our protest. The EU representative stuck stubbornly to his position and ended the conversation abruptly, saying that he and his colleagues would deal with things from there. He emphasized that, in any case, it was the Moroccan authorities who had the last word.

I was very disappointed by the outcome of this meeting. I couldn't stop thinking about the ordeal the migrants were enduring in Oujda. I called the UNHCR representative, who asked me if I could make contact with a Moroccan association that looked after migrants in Oujda, and implement a strategy that might allow the refugees and asylum seekers to return to Rabat. This I did: it enabled the few people with UNHCR papers to return to the capital. The rest of the migrants remained in Oujda. They managed to cope somehow, and were able to make their way back to Rabat several weeks later.

| MY CERTIFICATE OF RECOGNITION

Our efforts to establish good contacts with the students and overcome their prejudices against refugees and migrants had borne fruit, and on June 30, 2007, the DRC's independence day, we were invited to the university for the annual gala, where I had again been asked to speak. It was always a great honor for me to be able to speak on this occasion. Patrice Émery Lumumba paid for Congolese independence with his life, and every year, June 30 is a particularly important day for us.

At the end of the conference, several Congolese men and women were honored for their outstanding service to the community and presented with a certificate of recognition. Two people had already been called up when I unexpectedly heard my name. I was summoned to the podium and acknowledged with the following words: "We want to honor Emmanuel Mbolela for the extraordinary services he has rendered to sub-Saharan refugees and migrants. He has fought tirelessly for the rights of the sans-papiers. For this work, and for his support for our activities, we wish to present him, too, with our certificate of recognition."

What a pleasant surprise! Not only had we succeeded in gaining the respect of our student brothers and sisters—now they were honoring our work, as well. I was very moved, and felt greatly bolstered by this gesture of recognition. The certificate encouraged me to advocate even more for the interests of the community.

| DEPARTURE

Toward the end of 2007, I was in the middle of distributing invitations for an ARCOM conference in the G5 district of Rabat when I received a call from Lisa, a UNHCR employee. She invited me to come to the UNHCR building at 5:00 p.m. I agreed, and went to her office at the appointed time. I was extremely surprised when she told me what the UNHCR was offering me. There was a resettlement program for a very limited number of people, in the Netherlands. Lisa handed me a form to sign if I was interested. A thousand thoughts flashed through my mind. Over time, my life in Morocco had become increasingly unbearable. I was forced to live like a prisoner. Despite my status as a UNHCR-registered refugee, I could neither work nor travel abroad, so I was always prohibited from accepting the numerous invitations I had received from foreign human rights organizations over the years. After all this time, after all these battles, I was still stuck in Morocco. I had to accept the offer! But at the same moment, I thought that I couldn't just go and leave the community of sub-Saharan migrants here in Morocco in the lurch. My mind filled with images from our joint protests outside the UNHCR. I kept thinking of all the campaigns we had launched: to free prisoners, or get deportees back from Oujda. My thoughts were also with the many sick people we had supported and helped look after. I thought of our political campaigns against the raids. I pictured our school project, and all the children I'd picked up, day after day, and taken to class. All these thoughts made me feel terribly guilty. It would not be easy to leave behind the people with whom I had fought these battles. Lisa told me I had to make a quick decision. What answer should I give her?

She could see that I was hesitating. "I know what a huge gap your departure will leave in the refugee and migrant community," she said. "Many of your people won't be pleased about it." But as she said this, she pushed the form under my nose. I signed.

Two months later, Lisa called me again. I headed to the UNHCR office with mixed feelings. Lo and behold, my application had been accepted. I didn't know whether to laugh or cry.

It was another week before I received a call from a different UNHCR employee. I was to go to the Dutch embassy, and to take passport photos so they could issue me with a visa. At the embassy there were seven other refugees, including two couples and two children. Malou, the secretary of ARCOM, was also among those selected for the resettlement program, and he was waiting for me. We were very puzzled, and turned to the UNHCR employee, who was also present—"There are only eight of us? There'll be others coming, too, won't there?" But I was sadly mistaken. The Netherlands was taking just eight refugees.

My grief for my friends who would be left behind in Morocco was indescribable.

Over time, I managed to set this grief aside and slowly accustom myself to the idea of going to Europe. In time, I was even able to feel pleasure at this new development. I saw that the momentum that had accumulated through the self-organization of refugees and migrants would continue without me, too. Our movement had already demonstrated its effectiveness. There was great organizational and political knowledge in our ranks, and I was convinced that sooner or later the fight would be won and we would emerge victorious. I thought of Raoul and Astrid, who would assume the leadership of ARCOM. I also thought of the passionate activists Fiston Massamba and Pastor Willy Bayanga from the Council of Sub-Saharan Migrants in Morocco; of Fabien Didier Yene* and Louis Edongue from the Cameroonian migrant organization ADESCAM; of Marcel Amyeto; of the refugee women from the feminist organization COFESVIM, and of so many more . . . I thought of all the associations and groups supporting us in our struggle—the network Manifeste Euro-Africain and many others. I will never forget how they supported us in our protests against the deportations. All these thoughts went through my head as I prepared for my departure. I told myself that one day our voices would surely be heard.

And indeed—in 2013, for the first time in its history, Morocco implemented a process of legalization. Many sans-papiers received residence permits. All our years of perseverance paid off.

On the day of my departure, my friends and I shed a lot of

---

*See Fabien Didier Yene, *Bis an die Grenzen: Chronik einer Migration* (Klagenfurt, Austria: Drava Verlag, 2011).

tears. Many of those I was closest to said to me, "Emmanuel, wherever you go, don't forget our struggle! Don't forget us!"

At 9:00 a.m. on April 1, 2008, I boarded a Royal Air Maroc Boeing 777. As the plane ascended into the sky, I looked down at the ground below me and said, "Goodbye, Morocco! Living here was an experience I will never forget!"

7

EUROPE

From that Boeing 777, on April 1, 2008, I set eyes on European soil for the first time. As we approached Amsterdam's Schiphol Airport I gradually made out more details, and observed the differences from Africa. The first thing that struck me was all the bicycles, which were parked everywhere imaginable. I saw big freeways and neat houses. I could already tell that the surrounding landscape was beautiful. Malou, who was sitting close by, called over to me, "Preso [President], we're arriving in Europe!," and took a picture of me on the plane. The other passengers looked at us as if we were from the moon.

We landed a few minutes later. The pilot announced that the temperature outside was five degrees Celsius. In Morocco it had been eighteen degrees.

At the airport, we were warmly received by an employee of the IOM, the International Organization for Migration. This could hardly have been more ironic: in Morocco I had fought against the IOM, as it campaigned for the so-called "voluntary return" of migrants. I clearly recalled a debate at the Fondation Orient-Occident in Rabat, where I had argued with an IOM representative who had made the case for "voluntary return." I spoke against it, saying that this program was nothing more than the externalization of EU border protection by other means. You couldn't shatter the dreams of someone who wanted to go to Europe and then say it was "voluntary," I said. My intervention had sparked a long debate. And now, here in Amsterdam, I was being greeted by the IOM, of all things!

After going through customs, we were brought to Amersfoort, a town about two hours from Amsterdam, where the processing center for asylum seekers is based. Here, too, we were warmly welcomed. I had the impression that everything had already been prepared for us. One of the center's employees gave us a letter of welcome and the keys for our rooms. José—the musician friend with whom I had first come to Morocco—and I were given a room with a bunk bed. When we got to our room, we closed the door behind us and said our prayers. This time we didn't pray for God's help, as we had done so often in the desert. Nor did we pray for God to show us the way out of this vale of tears—rather, it was a prayer of thanks for the help and protection God had granted us on our long and arduous journey. Because only now were we truly able to say: our lives have been saved!

The fact that I had now finally gotten to Europe also brought so many questions with it. Now that my life was safe, would I be capable of establishing a new existence? Everything was new and unfamiliar: the language, the culture, the people I met. Was the Netherlands really a country where justice prevailed, somewhere I would be able to continue my political struggle? Was it possible to campaign for the rights of refugees and migrants here without fear of reprisals? All these questions haunted me until at last I fell asleep.

| MY NEW CIRCUMSTANCES

After spending three months in the processing center in Amersfoort, I found an apartment in Nunspeet, a small tourist town about fifty kilometers away. I completed all the formalities and headed for my new home, where in many respects I had to start again from scratch. I had painted my idea of my future in brighter colors; now, the sky above me darkened again. I was the only Congolese person in this neighborhood. There were two other African families, one from Burundi and one from Sudan, but none of these people spoke French. My neighbor across the corridor was a woman of about seventy who hardly ever left her room. The second neighbor on my floor was a man of about sixty who went to work in the morning, came home in the evening, and went straight to his apartment without speaking to anyone. Above me lived another elderly lady, whom I hardly ever saw. It was extremely strange for me to eat alone. In Africa, everyone eats together! Even if there's very little food, people come together and share whatever they have. In my family, it was usual to have a large number of people sitting around the table. We often had visitors—friends, brothers, sisters, nieces and nephews, cousins, or neighbors. It was impossible for outsiders to tell who was part of our immediate family and who wasn't. I experienced this practical solidarity again in Morocco, when we were all living together in the ghetto. Ten or more of us would be forced to live in a three-room apartment. We pooled whatever we had, and cooked together, as well. Those who didn't have money still got to eat, along with everyone else.

Now, suddenly, I was living in this lovely house surrounded

by a well-kept garden. The apartment offered me every comfort I could wish for. There was always lots to eat. But who was I to share my food with? I seriously wondered how people in Europe could bear to live like this. Is it material comforts and the development of modern communication technologies that have led people down this path of individualism and isolation? Will all people on Earth live like this in the future?

It was only after two weeks that I received my first visitor, a member of the local church. But he didn't understand French, either, and certainly not Tshiluba or Lingala—only Dutch. Luckily, we had studied Dutch for a few weeks at the refugee center, so I was able to communicate with my visitor at a very basic level. The man spoke the local dialect, so we could only converse about the simplest of things. It was twenty minutes before I understood that Cees, as he was called, was trying to explain to me where he'd gotten my contact details. On his second visit, he brought a translator along, which made things a whole lot easier. Thanks to Cees, I subsequently got to know the Zondag family, who helped me a great deal as I found my feet in Holland. They were nice, generous, and respectful people who supported me throughout my time in Nunspeet.

| CHALLENGES OF DAILY LIFE

Three months after I moved to Nunspeet, the parish assigned me a place at a language school in Harderwijk, about ten kilometers from the village. I was in a class with migrants from Afghanistan, Iraq, Colombia, Turkey, Morocco, and several Eastern European countries. Some had been living in the Netherlands for five years already, some for as long as ten.

———

I came to realize that, in general, the life of a refugee here in Europe was often far from easy. One day I met a nineteen-year-old African boy at the station who was shivering from head to toe with cold. He told me he had just come from Germany, and had had to spend the night in the open. I immediately took him to a store, where I bought him warm clothes and shoes. Then I brought him home with me and cooked him a hot meal. He told me he had lived in a refugee center in Germany for three years and that now they wanted to deport him, so he had fled to the Netherlands. He'd wanted to try to get to Eindhoven, where a friend of his lived, but he hadn't had enough money, so the conductor had made him get off the train. I accompanied the boy back to the station, and bought him a ticket to Eindhoven.

Here in the Netherlands, though, I started to realize that we sub-Saharan Africans were not the only ones fleeing, or leaving their country in search of a better life. At the language school, I met an Afghan who told me he had been in the Netherlands for ten years, and still had to live in a refugee center. He hadn't been able to look for work in all that time because he didn't have papers.

Not long after starting the language course, I had a bike accident and broke my left shoulder. There was snow on the ground that day, the first time since my arrival. I couldn't yet gauge how slippery and dangerous it was, and set off for the station on my bicycle as I did every day. Before I knew it, I was lying on the ground. People just walked past, looking at me passively as I picked myself up off the asphalt. *Here in Europe it's every*

man for himself. You fall over, and no one helps you up. Every-
one's in a hurry to get to their destination. That's just how it is!
I thought to myself, and cycled on to the station. It wasn't until
about 11:00 a.m. that I realized my shoulder was becoming increasingly painful. I could hardly participate in the class, it hurt
so much. When I got home at midday, I called Barta, my contact
person at the Dutch Council for Refugees. She went with me to
the hospital, where they put me in a cast. Barta looked after me
until the bones had healed and the plaster could come off again.

Learning Dutch was still a high priority for me. The language course wasn't enough. I went to the municipal volunteer
service and asked if there was a job they could give me, something I could do on a voluntary basis so I could learn Dutch more
quickly. The official there was very friendly and approachable.
She promised not only to arrange for me to work in a retirement
home, but also to find me a language tutor who would come to
me once a week.

At the retirement home, my job was to take coffee and tea
to people in their rooms. The work really helped me get to
know other cultures and the realities of other lives. At home in
the DRC, as in most African countries, parents do everything
to ensure that their children have a good life. Then, when the
parents are old and in need of care, it's the children who look
after them. If one of the two parents dies, the other moves in
with the children. Very often, young children are lucky enough
to be able to live with their grandparents. They love telling them
stories and playing with them. Boys and girls will often talk to
their grandparents about difficult subjects that they don't want
to discuss with their parents. What a huge difference from this
country! Here, people lived out their last days and years in retirement homes.

The conversations and exchanges with the pensioners there were very instructive for me. There were some sad moments, too. It sometimes happened I'd have a particularly nice conversation with someone, and then the person died a few days later. I remember Mrs. X., with whom I used to have regular chats. We liked each other very much. One day she didn't want to eat or drink anything anymore. I was very worried about her. Sure enough, the next day she was no longer there. I didn't have a chance to say goodbye.

I was constantly questioning my future in the Netherlands. My language skills were slowly improving, but the thing that bothered me most was the perpetual isolation from others. I had no opportunity to chat with my family or anyone from my country, or to make plans for the future. Congolese diplomas were not recognized here. This was a particularly bitter blow, because I had had to make a tremendous effort and invest so much money in order to study in Mbuji-Mayi. The only option open to me was to look for a Dutch school where I could study for a Dutch diploma. But for that I needed money. What could I do? After some time, my Internet research yielded results: I came across an organization called UAF, which awarded university grants for refugees. I registered with them, and to my surprise I received a positive response just a few days later. I could enroll at a university in Amsterdam—but of course this also meant that I had to move there.

Moving to Amsterdam was not an easy thing to do. The real estate companies' procedures seemed to me absurdly slow-moving and bureaucratic. After looking for a whole year, I was still living in Nunspeet.

One day, I met Mathias, a young African, at the local train station. He'd come to Nunspeet for a job interview, and asked me for directions. We hit it off, and exchanged phone numbers. A few months later, Mathias called me and said he'd gotten the job in Nunspeet. Now he had to move there from Dordrecht, and he needed an apartment. In the course of the conversation, it turned out that it would be in both our interests simply to swap apartments. He could live and work in Nunspeet, and I could live in Dordrecht—a significantly bigger city where there were more opportunities to find community—and go to university. It was no sooner said than done. And so I moved—not to Amsterdam, but I had gotten a little closer to achieving my goals.

| LOOKING FOR WORK

I started to look for work, applying not only in Dordrecht but also in several of the nearby towns and villages. However, the reaction from job agencies was usually not very encouraging: "The only work we have is for people with qualifications." The number of times I heard this sentence! Usually they didn't even ask about my education, and when I did once get as far as showing them my CV, I was told that I had no experience on the Dutch job market, and they couldn't place me for that reason. I was almost at my wits' end.

After some time, I finally found work at a garbage dump. Only migrants worked there. They came from Poland, Somalia, Morocco, Algeria, and Suriname. We worked in extremely dubious hygiene conditions, and were constantly exposed to the risk of picking up infections from the garbage. On my first day, I was given a jacket someone else had used before me; it stank terribly. I was also given a face mask that wasn't fit for the purpose; after just a few hours, you might as well have been working without one. We were only allowed to ask for a new one every three days. There were holes in the gloves we were given, which meant we inevitably came into contact with toxic liquids. During my first day at work, which lasted from 6:30 a.m. until 3:00 p.m., I was so nauseous that I couldn't eat or drink. When I got home after work, my whole body itched, and my clothes stank appallingly of garbage.

I struggled through the working days in the hope that I would grow accustomed to the job. However, by the end of the first week I had such difficulty breathing that I wasn't sure I should continue. Many of my colleagues had the same problem. The wages were as bad as the working conditions. Also, you had to work a three-week trial period before you could sign a contract, which was then only valid for three months, with the possibility of a single extension of another three months. I wondered whether I would even make it as far as signing the contract. And if I did, would they give me an extension? All these things were hugely concerning for me and my colleagues. Our precarious working conditions and the constant insecurity took a heavy toll on us, and people had different strategies for dealing with the situation. One man was always ranting furiously about our boss and wishing him all manner of ill. He told me that he himself had been living in Europe as an undocumented migrant for fifteen years, and his whole life was ruined. Another man would try to keep his spirits up by constantly joking around and performing little sketches to distract us from the cares of work. Some people laughed at his gags; others just thought he was crazy.

I went on working at the garbage dump, but I was constantly looking for another job. Before the three-week trial period was up, I actually got a call from an employment agency. I'd left my CV with them some time earlier. They now told me I could start work immediately at a vegetable packing company. It was a requirement of the job that I work Saturdays and Sundays as well. I also had to be contactable twenty-four hours a day, so I could be flexible about taking on shifts. It was a six-month limited contract, and the company was in a different town. These conditions weren't ideal, either, and I didn't know what to expect of the place, but I wanted to escape the garbage dump at all costs. I accepted the offer.

And so I started work at a big packing plant. My employer specialized in the buying, selling, and preserving of fruit and vegetables, and supplied a number of large supermarket chains in the Netherlands.

I started my new job on a Saturday. Here, too, the workforce was multinational: I had colleagues from sub-Saharan Africa, the Maghreb, Asia, and Latin America. My first impression was that there was a good atmosphere among the workers. Almost everyone had someone they could talk to in their mother tongue, and I, too, found a number of people at the company with whom I could speak Lingala.

However, my first day at work was a real baptism by fire. We'd been working at the machines since 8:30 a.m., and we didn't know when we would be sent home. Beside me on the production line was a young man from Curaçao. He'd been at the company for two months already, so he was fairly experienced. We'd been assigned to pack tomatoes. My job was to empty the crates and put them away. The crates were heavy, and although I picked up two at once, my colleague called over to me that I had to take four if we were to get through the forty pallets assigned to us. There was no way I could carry four crates at once, so I did my best to struggle along with three. When we'd finished packing the required forty pallets, more goods were suddenly brought and the work continued. It was 8:00 p.m. before we were allowed a proper break. We'd been promised something to eat, but we weren't given anything. The workers started whispering among themselves, but no one dared to raise their voice and call for an end to the working day. We knew that our contracts required us to work weekends for as long as it took to reach the production target. After fifteen minutes, we were called back to the machines. We shuffled over to the crates of vegetables. Everyone looked exhausted. Three quarters of an hour later, our food finally arrived. We were permitted another break of thirty minutes. Our working day didn't finish until 10:30 p.m. Dog-tired, we dragged ourselves to the cloakrooms in silence.

I got home around midnight and slept like a log, but I had to be up again at five in the morning to be at work punctually at 8:30 a.m., when the drudgery began all over again. That day, we had to work even harder than the previous one. The work finished at 8:00 p.m., and this time we didn't even get anything to eat. The boss actually tried to make us work longer, but the majority of workers refused.

These two days showed me what I could expect if I stayed in this job. After careful consideration I decided that, for the time being, I would stay.

The big problem with the rhythm of work in this factory was the packing machines. They dictated the speed of the process, and they were merciless. One day, I was working on a machine known as "Bordes." A Polish colleague who had been there a long time warned me that the work on this machine was particularly demanding. "You usually need more people to operate it, too," he added. I'd been assigned to work on it alone. My colleague tried to encourage me. I was sweating profusely and finding it really hard to lift the package crates. When the bell sounded for the break, I was completely worn out.

Some workers did their very best and really wanted to do things well—but the working atmosphere was marred by our boss's despotic behavior. He was always breathing down our necks and ordering us around, as if he were a colonial master from some bygone age. His behavior provoked resentment among the workers and resulted in tensions that sometimes erupted into violence. Once, the boss went so far as to send a group of people home just for talking to one another on the production line.

Another time, I witnessed a furious row between an older male colleague and a younger female one. They were standing beside each other at a packing machine. The young woman was working so fast that the older man couldn't keep up, and in his distress he started yelling at her. But the poor woman couldn't help it—she was afraid the boss wouldn't extend her contract if she worked too slowly. All this reminded me of my comrade in arms Lucile Dumas, an activist with ATTAC Maroc. She'd campaigned on behalf of the Moroccan women toiling away on Spanish tomato plantations. Ironically, the tomatoes we were packing that day were imported from Spain.

Everyone suffered under these working conditions. One day, at the end of a long, hard week, we were in the changing cubicles when a colleague remarked, "This goddamn job! We've just worked through the night, every night for a week, for a pittance.

I checked my bank balance today. It made me and my kids want to weep!"

The colleague sitting next to him was equally outraged. "If the boss asks me to work through the night one more time, I'm going to give him an earful!" he cried. "Not only have we just worked through the night five days in a row, we also had to work on Sunday! For this terrible pay!" They were both absolutely right. And their wages were higher than mine, as they'd already been working for the company for six months, and I was still new. Sometimes I would work eight hours and only be paid for seven!

The company usually informed us of our shift times by text message. And, like a bad joke, we received a text message from the boss that day, saying: "Thank you, everyone! Top performance this week! More than 175,000 cartons of tomato soup were packed. That's the most we've ever managed!"

The working conditions in this factory were, without doubt, extremely hard on all of us. Nonetheless, I tried to use the time, as best I could, to actively observe the social reality in which I found myself. I compared the conditions here in the Netherlands with what I'd heard about Europe all those years ago, on Place Tchad in Tamanrasset. I tried to talk to as many of my colleagues as possible and find out their stories. Most of them were migrants, like me. During breaks, or on the train journeys to and from work, we would chat about all sorts of things, and I heard a lot about their migration histories. Many of them cursed their countries' governments and blamed them for their hard life in exile. Once, I was traveling home from work with an African colleague. We had just worked through the night, and my colleague had gotten into an argument with the boss. He was absolutely furious, and it was as if he wanted to vent his irritation on me. "The reason we're suffering here is the terrible governance in our own countries!" he ranted. "Back home, our minimum wage is barely a hundred and fifty euros a month. Our president stands there crowing about how we've supposedly got billions of dollars in foreign currency reserves—and all the while the population is suffering! You understand me? All we have is corruption. The bastards who lead the country share out all the revenue from the oil business among themselves and a few foreign companies!"

But while some directed their anger at the governments back in our home countries, others started to complain about their own brothers and sisters. Once, when we were sitting together, a colleague from the DRC said, "Look how we're slaving away here! What are our people doing back home in the meantime? We send them money, and instead of investing it they throw it out the window with both hands! They think here in Europe money grows on trees!"

A Guinean colleague agreed. "Yes, my friend, that's just how it is! I'm sick to death of my countrymen! How many times have I sent money home—I've even shipped goods over from Europe and traveled to Guinea to set up a small company. It was all fine as long as I was there, but once I came back to the Netherlands nothing worked properly at home anymore. People don't understand that things in Europe are quite different to what they imagine. We work and work, and we only ever see our wages on our bank statements. They deduct everything straight away: taxes, electricity bills, rent. What's left over for us?" A third colleague added that he had to take care of his whole extended family in Africa before he could even think about covering his own costs.

I commented that the root of the problem was that the generation that had come to Europe before us had always boasted back home about how well they were doing in Europe. They always had to show that they had made it. To admit failure was a big disgrace.

It was good to be constantly exchanging views, to discuss things and argue about them. What impressed me most, undoubtedly, was the stamina, perseverance, and solidarity of all these people who, in spite of the difficulties, supported their families in Africa for years on end. They transferred money so their sister or brother could study, paid the rent their parents couldn't afford, sent medicines for sick family members or childhood friends. It was as if the sub-Saharan migrants in Europe had assumed the responsibilities that their governments back home should have fulfilled. "The day we stop sending money home," I said to a friend one day, "will be the day the people's uprising against our governments begins."

But it was clear to me that we here in Europe had to organize, too. In addition to my everyday struggles at the factory and in society, I wanted finally to go back to university, to continue my education and hone my critical faculties. Six months later, my contract expired and was not renewed—the kind of insecurity that all migrants constantly face. I remember the words of my colleague: "We've succeeded in getting to Europe; now we have to fight." Yes: for us migrants, Europe is a daily battle, one we have to engage in on every level. That was why, after I moved to Dordrecht, I decided to go back to school. For two years I commuted between Dordrecht and Amsterdam, where I studied at the Amsterdam University of Applied Sciences. At the same time, I also got involved with the network Afrique-Europe-Interact.*

| ACTIVISM IN EUROPE

"Emmanuel, don't forget us! Wherever you go, fight for our rights!" I will never forget the words said to me at my farewell party in Rabat. The extent of my responsibility toward my friends in Morocco was clear to me; people back home in the DRC also had high expectations of me. My family, my friends, and above all my comrades in arms hoped I would continue to campaign for fundamental political change. "Things are bad here in the DRC. The country urgently needs people like you!" they told me on the phone.

But there was plenty to do here in Europe, too. I could see that the situation of undocumented migrants was disastrous in every country on the continent. Their most fundamental rights were denied them, and all the while the EU claimed to be a guarantor of human rights.

From the DRC to Morocco to Europe—I wanted to, had to, stay active and keep fighting for a fair and equitable society. Little by little, I got to know groups and initiatives with whom I could work. Over the following years I traveled through many countries, participated in conferences and protest actions, and shared all my experiences. I didn't only speak about the situation of migrant men and women; I also tried to enlighten the

*www.afrique-europe-interact.net

European public about the reasons why people migrate, or flee their countries. I gave many lectures about armed conflicts in Africa, the pillaging of natural resources, and, of course, about our despotic governments, as well as about the ongoing political support they received from Europe.

On June 11, 2008, just two months after I arrived in the Netherlands, I spoke before a large audience in Europe for the first time. It was a welcome relief in contrast to the hard work and isolation of my life at the time. The human rights organizations LOS and All Included had invited me to Amsterdam for a conference about the murderous practices of the border protection agency Frontex. We discussed what could be done about the EU's closed-door policy. I had the opportunity to speak about the disastrous situation of refugees and migrants before an audience of European citizens. Naturally, I didn't fail to mention that the EU played a large part in all this, and that the Maghreb countries received money from Europe to take action against so-called "illegals."

At this conference I also met Rian, the coordinator of LOS, and Vincent, who works with All Included. We immediately hit it off. Both organizations campaign for global freedom of movement and are very active in supporting refugees and migrants. A banner with the slogan "No human being is illegal" was rolled out in front of the office of All Included. This slogan perfectly summarized the group's political approach. I felt invigorated and strengthened in my aims. At this conference, I decided to use my legal status in the Netherlands to campaign on behalf of those who did not have this privilege, and were falsely designated "illegals."

After this conference I was invited to an antiracism camp in Hamburg. I presented another lecture about the situation in Morocco at a workshop about migration, and gave an interview to the local radio station. It was another opportunity to meet many like-minded people. I would like to mention that I have Conni Gunsser from the Hamburg Refugee Council to thank for the invitation to this camp. I knew Conni from Oujda; we'd both participated in a memorial service there in 2005, after the events in Ceuta and Melilla. I learned a lot from her about the situation of refugees and migrants in Germany. In many respects, it seemed to be similar to that of my friends in Morocco.

When I got back to the Netherlands, I found an invitation to attend the World Social Forum on Migration, which was to take place in Madrid in September 2008. I accepted immediately—after all, the Forum is one of the most important international gatherings of all the political groups working on this topic. Thousands of people met to discuss the global economy, climate change, armed conflicts, and of course the situation of refugees and migrants. The forum was entitled: "Our Voices, Our Rights: For a World Without Walls." At the event, I talked about the fences in Ceuta and Melilla that separate Africa from Europe. My speech was outshone by that of Victor Nzuzi, an exemplary activist who is also from the DRC. Ever since that forum in Madrid, I have always admired Victor for his political and rhetorical skill. In every one of his speeches he manages to explain, in a way that's easy to grasp, why the fight for global freedom of movement and the fight against neocolonial exploitation inevitably go hand in hand.

Then, in October 2008, I was invited to Paris to take part in the conference "Des Ponts, Pas Des Murs," organized by Migreurop in collaboration with the group Manifeste Euro-Africain.

This became one of the highlights of my career as an activist. I spoke at a big event on the place de la République, where I stood in for my Moroccan colleague Hicham Rachidi, who had had to travel on to Lyon that evening. Thousands of people had shown up, from many different European and African countries. I stepped onto the podium, and saw before me the monument commemorating the French Revolution, with its famous allegorical statues representing "Liberty—Equality—Fraternity." Inspired by the statues, I cried, "Liberty, not arrests! Equality, not discrimination! Fraternity, not racism!"

This book was published first in German in 2014, in French in 2016, and in Italian in 2018. Since then, along with Alexander Behr, who translated the book into German, I have organized more than four hundred conferences in Germany, Austria, France, Italy, Luxembourg, the Netherlands, Portugal, and Switzerland. They have been very well received everywhere.

All the international meetings, conferences, and protest actions I have participated in over the years have fundamentally changed my life. I was pleased and proud to become acquainted with a world of solidarity, and to have the opportunity to experience another culture of personal interaction. The exchange with other activists on the subject of international migration was always of central importance to me.

After the four long years stuck in Morocco, now at last I could do what I wanted to do—what I saw as my mission. I had received a number of invitations while I was still living in Morocco, but my visa applications were always rejected. Every time I would wait for an answer from the respective embassy, only to be rejected—yet the costs for the visa application were never reimbursed.

| INVOLVEMENT WITH AFRIQUE-EUROPE-INTERACT

One day I received a call from Conni Gunsser in Hamburg. She invited me to a meeting in Bremen, where activists from Germany and other European countries were meeting up with refugees and migrants who had organized themselves. I agreed, and went along.

I was very excited by the dynamism of this meeting. Many of those present had already known each other a long time, and had worked together in various different networks over the years. They had gone on No Border camps together, and had demonstrated against the G8 summit in Heiligendamm in 2007. Some of them were part of the No Lager network, which had organized a lot of campaigns against the terrible accommodations for refugees and migrants in Germany. Consequently, I had already met some of them at the antiracism camp in Hamburg in 2008. In short—the attendees possessed a wealth of experience of fighting against racism and discrimination, against borders, and against neocolonial and capitalist conditions.

I was also delighted that every participant was given space at the meeting to present his or her views. What affected me most, though, was the report by a group of migrant men and women about their living conditions in a German refugee camp. Among other things, they reported that people living in camps like these were forbidden to leave the place they were in without authorization from the asylum authorities. I had not expected to hear such things here in Germany, the country where the fall of the Berlin Wall had been such an important milestone for freedom of movement. I was also moved by the report by Riadh Ben

Ammar, a migrant from Tunisia who had managed to get documented in Germany. He told me how he had come to Europe without papers and had had to sleep out in the open for nights on end, in the middle of winter. He had also passed through the Netherlands on his journey. He had been threatened directly with deportation on many occasions. "All the things I had to go through finally to get papers!" he said to me. "This experience has taught me that we should never give up the fight!"

A few months later I traveled to Jena with the people from the Bremen meeting, where we participated in an antiracism festival. It was called "United Against Colonial Injustice, In Memory of the Dead of Fortress Europe," and was organized by the "Caravan for the Rights of Refugees and Migrants."* Around a thousand people had come. This meeting wasn't just about developing common strategies to overcome European border policy—the aim was also to remind Europe of the negative consequences that the colonization of Africa continues to have today.

At this festival, we also had a meeting with Ousmane Diara and Alassane Dicko, two activists from the Malian Association for Deportees (AME).† We talked to them about establishing a transnational network in order better to coordinate our activities in West Africa and Europe. So it was that we eventually founded Afrique-Europe-Interact (AEI). Since then, the network has united grassroots antiracism groups from Mali, Togo, Burkina Faso, the DRC, Germany, Austria, and the Netherlands. The aim is to facilitate an exchange between African and European activists, and to carry out joint campaigns. One thing

---

*See www.karawane-festival.org and www.thecaravan.org.
†See www.expulsesmaliens.info.

that's particularly important to us is to collaborate on an equal footing—which is a big challenge, given the huge prosperity gap between the two continents. AEI champions global freedom of movement and equitable development. The network's activities cannot be compared with those of a charitable NGO—instead, the idea is that refugees and migrants living in Europe should speak for themselves. In the African countries where AEI is active, its purpose is to get emergency aid to migrants who have been deported from Europe. It also aims to provide them with a political platform through which to represent their interests.

The first big action by Afrique-Europe-Interact took place in January and February 2011, when a bus caravan was organized to drive from Bamako, the capital of Mali, to Dakar, the capital of Senegal. The caravan's final destination was the World Social Forum in Dakar. Around three hundred activists from African and European countries took part. A particularly important role was played by self-organized refugees and migrants of African origin who had succeeded in obtaining documentation in Europe, and who were now participating in the Forum. I was proud to be part of this group. We traveled through many villages and towns in Mali and Senegal, talking to the local population about migration, freedom of movement, and development. Along the route, which was more than 1,300 kilometers, we held a series of exciting discussion events. Another subject we addressed was that of land-grabbing—the mass selling-off of fertile farmland to transnational concerns and investment companies.

When we arrived in Dakar, I represented Afrique-Europe-Interact at a conference on the island of Gorée, at which the International Migrant Charter was drawn up. The conference took place ahead of the Social Forum, and migrants from all over the world took part. The island of Gorée, within sight of Dakar, was chosen as the location for this meeting because of its great historical significance. Under the colonizers, Gorée served as an assembly point for the countless slaves who were then carried off to America. The history of the island is therefore symbolic of the dehumanization of people, of mass forced labor, and of the indescribable suffering of countless men, women, and children. This was precisely the reason why this place was selected for the proclamation of the Migrant Charter: it was to give the island of Gorée a new significance, emphasizing human beings' unassailable dignity.

After that, the Social Forum was held on the campus of Dakar University. We, the members of the caravan, participated by holding a series of workshops and podium discussions. At the end, there was a big demonstration of about a thousand people outside the Frontex office in Dakar. During this demonstration, something remarkable happened. A Senegalese policeman came up to me and said in confidence: "Brother, what you're doing here is really encouraging for us. Finally, someone dares to speak the truth, loudly and clearly. I hope the political decision makers will finally change course . . ."

We weren't the only caravan that had traveled to the Social Forum. There was a big group that had come from Nigeria, and another . . . from Morocco. So it was that I was finally able to see some of my friends from Rabat again. It was a moment of great joy.

Altogether, this first big operation by Afrique-Europe-Interact lasted more than three weeks, and after this, links between activists on the two continents were even closer than before.

| AFRIQUE-EUROPE-INTERACT AND THE
ARAB SPRING

The great wave of political transformation in the Arab world that started in Tunisia in 2010 and subsequently spread to Egypt, Libya, and other countries of the region prompted us to extend the radius of our activities. In June 2011, a delegation from Afrique-Europe-Interact drove to Tunisia to establish contact with activists there. The delegation was intended to express our solidarity with the Tunisian people, who had just achieved a successful revolution. The group also traveled to the refugee camp of Choucha in the southeast of the country, which at the time was housing thousands of refugees from Libya.

The report the delegation brought us was very alarming. The Libyan refugees were able to return to their country relatively soon after the death of Muammar al-Gaddafi, but the sub-Saharan migrants who had fled Libya were now stuck in Choucha. Although most of them had been living and working in Libya for years, it was now absolutely impossible for them to return. They were accused of having fought as mercenaries for Gaddafi, and were in grave danger of being targeted in pogroms. But they were also in danger in Choucha. The local population repeatedly attacked the camp, and once again, the UNHCR, which should have been responsible for the refugees' security, proved itself incapable of protecting them. The European Union turned a deaf ear and refused to give the refugees safe passage to Europe. Many people from Choucha who tried to reach Italy in small boats drowned in the Mediterranean.

And it wasn't only sub-Saharan migrants who died. The 2011 revolution had encouraged tens of thousands of young

Tunisians to finally brave the crossing to Europe. Many of them did succeed in reaching Italy, but many thousands never arrived.

Faced with this alarming situation, Afrique-Europe-Interact decided to support the "Boats for People" campaign, which was staged in the summer of 2012. Our aim was to criticize the EU's murderous border policy with symbolic actions that would be effective in attracting publicity.

We started our campaign in Palermo, where we boarded the public ferry to Tunis. There were around a hundred activists from European and African countries. Once on board, we staged an unannounced event, during which we made passengers aware of our concerns. Equipped with flyers, a microphone, and a loudspeaker, we spoke about freedom of movement and the Arab Spring, in French, Italian, and Arabic. Our action was surprisingly well received, and lively discussions ensued. Tunisians who lived abroad and were traveling home for their holiday were especially interested in what we had to say. Over the following days, with the help of local activists and students, we organized a series of events and roundtable discussions.

On this trip, I tried to speak with as many Tunisians as I could and talk to them about their recent revolution. I had only followed the events of 2011 on television—now I had the opportunity to speak directly to the men and women who had achieved this revolution. I wanted to understand exactly how it had come about and what had driven people to make it happen. In all the conversations, I was always told that it had been a revolt that had started from the bottom up. I also learned that Ben Ali's despotic regime, under which they had all suffered so badly, had been supported by the West until the very last minute! Ben Ali's supposed economic achievements, which powerful countries had used to justify keeping the regime going, were all just propaganda. The spectacular high-rise buildings and the investments in large-scale infrastructure projects only served to disguise the poverty of the majority of the population. A Tunisian I spoke to near the kasbah in Tunis told me: "My friend, enough is enough! All of us in this country have worked our fingers to the bone, just so that one man and his family could become immeasurably rich! For several decades a small group of individuals divided all the wealth among themselves, while we suffered. They'd better not dare come back!"

All this reminded me horribly of the DRC, a country whose riches are commandeered by a small kleptocracy while the majority of the people are forced to live in misery. I understood that the dictators on the African continent all acted according to similar patterns. While the population starved and children couldn't go to school because teachers' salaries hadn't been paid, Mobutu had staged grandiose celebrations where people had to pay homage to his regime. These were the official images the DRC presented to the world. Mobutu wanted to give the impression that everything in his country was as good as possible. And the West used those images to justify its continued support for the dictator.

Despite the 2018 elections that installed the new president in the DRC, the situation in the country remains very precarious. Large-scale massacres of the population are currently taking place in the northeast of the country, specifically in the province of Beni. The key players of the former Kabila regime still call the shots.

After our stay in Tunis, we drove about six hundred kilometers south and visited the refugee camp of Choucha. At first we were denied entry to the camp. We couldn't help wondering whether this was to protect the refugees, or whether they wanted to prevent us from seeing the miserable living conditions in the camp for ourselves. Choucha is in the middle of the desert: temperatures can be as high as forty-five degrees Celsius, and drop below freezing in winter. The first thing we heard from the refugees was that there wasn't a single water point in the entire camp. Some of the people we met were determined that we should be allowed to see inside the tents. When at last we were allowed to enter them, our fears were confirmed. Many refugees had fallen sick because of the lack of drinking water. We saw a four-year-old girl who was fighting for her life after drinking water unfit for consumption. Yet in addition to all the terrible things we saw, I remarked upon the strength, resilience, and generosity of the people living there. They were destitute, yet despite this, one of them invited me into his tent and offered me a can of cola.

At the end of our trip we took part in a meeting of the social movements in the city of Monastir. I was still very affected by what I had just seen in Choucha. At the press conference organized by Boats for People, at which I, too, was to speak, I therefore tried to find a political answer to the Choucha crisis, and addressed the Tunisians directly. "The Tunisian revolution was a clear expression of the fact that there is a great longing for freedom and justice in this country," I said. "These are values to which the sub-Saharan refugees and migrants are also entitled. If we are fighting for freedom of movement in Europe and campaigning for the rights of the Tunisian immigrants, we cannot at the same time accept the rights of sub-Saharan refugees being trampled on here in Tunisia."

That trip to Tunisia in the summer of 2012 had a big impact on me. I was very impressed by the commitment of the activists from Afrique-Europe-Interact and their persistence in defending the rights of refugees and migrants. I was inspired by their concrete and practical interest in the reality on the African continent. However, it is important to make clear that the network's driving force comes from refugees and migrants themselves. They aren't just joining in; in most cases, they are the ones who come up with the ideas for campaigns. The majority of the activities of AEI's African section also originate from groups that are active in the region. One example is the variety of activities carried out by Malian grassroots movements, which are financially supported by AEI Europe, but conceived and implemented locally.

I feel strengthened in my commitment by the people who have joined me in finding practical solutions to the fundamental problems faced by refugee women and children at the gates of Europe, in countries which this same Europe designates safe in order that refugees can be confined there. I am thinking of those men and women whose commitment and financial support have enabled me to realize a project to house migrant women in Rabat, and to continue with the schooling of migrant children in Morocco. Since 2013, thanks to our efforts, the Moroccan authorities have accepted that the children of migrants should be admitted to Moroccan public schools. However, this decision made no difference, because the parents lack the means to purchase school supplies, pay for transport, or even buy food. This is why, with the support of many German, Austrian, and Swiss individuals, foundations, and organizations, we have set up a project to sponsor the integration of migrant children into Moroccan public schools. As well as integrating the children, our association also runs a center for educational support and literacy, where we welcome hundreds of women and children every Wednesday and Saturday.

The regime change that has taken place in my country provides us with a good opportunity to organize a transnational conference of social actors in Kinshasa to address the situation there. I took advantage of my visit to the DRC in the summer of 2019 to prepare for this major conference. The aim is to bring together Congolese social actors from both African and European countries to exchange and share their experiences and struggles. This would help to consolidate peace in the DRC and the Great Lakes subregion, and would at last create a bridge between African and European activists with a view to future cooperation and grassroots action.

For Afrique-Europe-Interact, the self-organization of those directly affected is paramount. And yet: the commitment of men and women from Europe in campaigning for changes to asylum and migration policy and continuing to protest against their governments will be very important for the future of Euro-African relations. In a way, the current situation can be compared to the period of decolonization. Back then, there were many Europeans who fought stubbornly against the African countries' attempts to gain their independence. Ultimately, however, the struggle of the Black peoples, which was supported by a minority in Europe, led to victory and independence becoming a reality. The same will be true of the implementation of global freedom of movement.

———

I think the approach AEI aims to establish, of cooperation on an equal footing between grassroots initiatives in Europe and in Africa, can serve as a model for other organizations. This policy should inspire not only NGOs and human rights groups, but also state, regional, and international organizations. It cannot still be acceptable for ready-made concepts that have nothing in common with African reality to be imposed on our countries. This applies to both traditional development aid and to European ideas of how democracy should look. In chapter 2, I wrote about how the infamous "1+4" government model was imposed on the DRC at the Inter-Congolese Dialogue in South Africa. The idea came not from the Congolese, but from the powerful countries of the north.

There are hundreds of extremely well-financed and well-equipped European organizations in Africa. But there is often a gulf between them and the local population. This is why it's important always to seek contact with grassroots initiatives that are familiar with the terrain and that know which political steps will be constructive and which will not. At the same time, however, there must in the future be guarantees that these organizations will be granted access to public funding as well, regardless of whether they are in sub-Saharan Africa, the Maghreb, or Europe.

EPILOGUE

THE BAOBAB: A REFUGE FOR MIGRANT WOMEN

I have reached the end of my story—the story of a political struggle that forced me to take the road into exile.

I hope that this book will contribute in some small way to making the voiceless heard, and to mobilizing even more people to challenge decision makers about the dramatic consequences of their xenophobic security policies. Thanks to the meetings organized around the German and French editions of this book, we at ARCOM, together with Afrique-Europe-Interact, were able to realize a project very dear to our hearts: the establishment of a house for migrant women in Rabat. At the various readings I did in Germany, Austria, France, Switzerland, and Luxembourg, we collected donations that enabled us to open this shelter specifically for migrant women arriving in Morocco. After crossing the Sahara desert, where the majority of them suffer atrocities, these women often arrive in Rabat knowing no one, not even knowing where they can sleep. They are sexually exploited by networks that take advantage of their situation, and sometimes even by men from their own communities. Many of them live by begging. They sleep in railway stations.

With the help of initial donations from two women, one in Germany, the other in Austria, I went to Morocco in February 2015, and, with ARCOM, opened a house for women. I named this center Le Baobab, because in my country—in my home-town, in particular—the foliage of the baobab tree offers restor-ative shade to hunters, who, after hunting all day and returning empty-handed, gather beneath it to rest, discuss, and redefine their strategies. In the same way, our center offers temporary and emergency accommodation to women who have just arrived in Rabat. It allows them to rest and recover their strength for three months, to talk about their experiences and redefine their future prospects. When we opened this center, it started out as an apartment for six women; however, the demand is so great that we have since expanded and now have seven apartments ca-pable of housing seventy to eighty women. This is still nowhere near enough. Since opening The Baobab, we have taken in many women of different nationalities. Priority is given to pregnant women and women accompanied by children.

The center is managed by my colleagues who founded ARCOM with me, as well as by other women who, after being taken in by the center, agreed to stay on and work with us. Most of the women who come to the center have never been to school. This is why we had the idea of organizing other activities there, such as literacy courses and vocational training.

Our little school, located in a working-class neighborhood of Rabat, welcomes not only the children of migrants but also those of Moroccans who are interested in learning French and English. Coeducation brings the children of migrants and the children of Moroccans together, which helps break down prejudices and combat racism.

In December 2018, Morocco hosted the Global Forum on

Migration and Development, which led to the adoption of the Global Compact on Migration. On the sidelines of this forum, ARCOM organized a transnational conference in Rabat that brought together more than four hundred people, mostly migrants living in Morocco, some activists and defenders of migrants' rights and freedoms from Europe (Germany, Austria, France, the Netherlands, and Switzerland), and others from Africa (Gabon, Mali, and Niger). The conference was titled "La Parole aux Migrant(e)s"—"Giving Migrants a Voice"—since they are the ones most affected by discriminatory policies and measures restricting the mobility of people, and yet they rarely have a platform to speak. It was also about strengthening transnational links between social movements, and creating bridges between Africa and Europe. A great many women participated in the conference, and I was moved by the fact that the women who spoke were not cowed by the restrictions and suffering of their lives in Morocco. Instead, they energetically insisted on their right to travel, and denounced colonial and neocolonial exploitation, Western leaders' support for African dictators, and the plundering of Africa's wealth, these being among the many reasons they were forced to take the path into exile. They were indignant about Europe closing the door on them, asking: What would Europe be without Africa? All this showed that migrant women do not want to be passive victims. They are fighting to change their situation, fighting for a better future. They don't want to remain submissive; they want to emancipate themselves from patriarchal and domestic violence. They want to live in freedom. This is the reason why they leave.

AFTERWORD: THE CURRENT SITUATION IN THE DRC

No African dictator can remain in power for long without the support of the West. This has been my consistent message at every conference I've spoken at these last five years.

As I put the finishing touches on the English edition of this book, my country has just passed a major turning point. The handover of power from Joseph Kabila, the outgoing president, to Félix Tshisekedi took place without bloodshed in January 2019. This is a first in the history of the Congo.

This changeover came about as a result of years of struggle on the part of the entire Congolese population. It is the culmination of the fight, begun by Patrice Émery Lumumba, for the full enfranchisement of the Congolese people. That fight cost the lives of thousands of my comrades, and forced me into exile. As I explained in chapter 1, the change of power in the DRC remains highly ambivalent. Nevertheless, this victory gives me a sense of pride, and helps heal the wounds I suffered as a result of my political engagement, and on my journey into exile.

For the record, Joseph Kabila remained in power for seventeen years, thanks to the support of Western governments that needed him to facilitate their international transactions. Kabila had already been defeated in all the elections of recent years, particularly in 2006 and 2011, but with the support of his Western sponsors he still managed to cling to power. I remember the elections of 2011. They were won by the late UDPS leader Étienne Tshisekedi, but Kabila had the advantage of external support, as well as the backing of the army and the police, which he used to maintain his imperium.

Over the past three years, however, Kabila lost this external support because of trade agreements he signed with China, allowing it to exploit mining rights for minerals. He tried repeatedly to introduce a bill that would revise the constitution in order to enable him to stand for a third term, but the populace took to the streets en masse, forcing parliament to reject the bill. Kabila played for time; elections were not held in 2016 as scheduled. However, the people continued to exert heavy pressure on him, calling for the organization of free and transparent elections. This pressure cost the lives of numerous demonstrators who were killed by police, and opposition activists were arrested and imprisoned. Ultimately, however, Kabila gave in, and elections were held two years later. The people made their choice: they voted Kabila out of office. A whole history led up to the making of this choice: the history of a people who did not abandon the fight when their independence was taken from them by the imperialists who assassinated Lumumba, the father of Congolese independence, the leader who envisioned the full enfranchisement of the Congolese people. Later, the Congolese people reorganized, throwing themselves once more into the struggle against the dictators whom the neocolonizers had forcibly installed. It is to this people that we owe the democratic and peaceful transfer of power which has just taken place in the DRC.

The current president has inherited a country that, more than half a century on from Lumumba's assassination, is in a disastrous, chaotic situation. He finds it at the bottom of the abyss. All the indicators—social, political, economic, and ecological—are flashing red. The tramping of combat boots is still heard in some of the country's eastern provinces. Epidemics of diseases such as Ebola and cholera are raging in some parts of the country; as I write, in 2020, COVID-19 is spreading around the globe, and it is obvious that countries with a poor health-care system, like the DRC, suffer most from this new disease. The UDPS's victory in the 2018 elections has often been questioned, and it has been said that Félix Tshisekedi is just a puppet of Kabila. However, knowing full well the UDPS's capacity for mobilization, Félix cannot be said to have been installed by Kabila to serve as his puppet. What is true is that, before he would agree to relinquish power, Kabila demanded guarantees of protection for himself and his clique. This is the sense in which there were negotiations between him and Félix. It is important to understand that if Félix moved too fast, he could ruin everything and run the risk of plunging the country back into war, which would claim many more lives. It must be remembered that all the intelligence services, the police, and the army were put in place by Kabila. The UDPS was in opposition for thirty-seven years; it was kept under such strict surveillance that it was impossible for the party to have any spies within the system. Clearly, the new president has inherited a delicate situation. Training and retraining is required at all levels; this takes time, and calls for dedicated strategies and resources.

To cut a long story short: The dignitaries who have had to

relinquish power still control the army, the police, and the security services; they are also still present in the various sectors of the country's economy. On top of this, they have acquired a majority in the parliament and the senate, in a manner that has yet to be clarified, with the sole aim of preventing the new president from making his mark and implementing social policies and programs that would meet the population's expectations.

Since coming to power, President Tshisekedi has ordered the release of political prisoners and opinion leaders. Public freedoms, such as freedom of expression and assembly, are guaranteed, although the attitudes and behavior of former dignitaries who are still preoccupied with their selfish interests are preventing the new authorities from working freely. The question is whether Félix Tshisekedi is strong enough, and willing, to oppose these old tendencies. At the end of April 2020, Human Rights Watch put out a press release in which they noted that the police still arbitrarily arrest and detain peaceful demonstrators. This undoubtedly creates confusion in people's minds, to the extent that some are starting to wonder about the future of the country following the change of leadership.

The domestic state of affairs is compounded by the regional and international situation. Since 1996, the DRC has been dealing with a war of depopulation and repopulation, the ultimate objective of which is the balkanization of the country. This war is being waged by militias backed by neighboring countries, including Burundi, Rwanda, and Uganda, which in turn are supported by certain multinational companies. At the same time, China's presence in Africa has alarmed the traditional colonial powers, and the DRC finds itself, as ever, at the center of this struggle for position, on account of its immense strategic mineral resources.

The question that haunts me, as it does the majority of the grassroots membership of our political party, the UDPS, is whether the new president will use his leadership to meet the demands of the rank and file, which are also those of the party's founding fathers; whether he will have the interests of the people at heart in everything he does, or whether the pleasures and comforts afforded by power might tempt him to slide into corruption, oppression, and all the evils we denounced during our years of struggle. When I visited the DRC in the summer of 2019, this was the question on the lips of the grassroots party members. They remain cautious and vigilant.

It is this, the people's expectation of real change, that will make it possible to reduce the ever-increasing inequalities between rich and poor. It will permanently guarantee the liberties and fundamental rights I await so eagerly, enabling me to return and live in my country alongside my brothers and sisters, friends and acquaintances, whom I met on my last visit to the DRC. They are waiting for me to come, so that together we can set up projects that will contribute to the reconstruction of our country.

I was in the DRC to get a sense of the situation on the ground after so many years away, and I am currently preparing to return. I had no problems at the airport when I went, and at this stage I can no longer say that anything is preventing me from going back. Things are starting to change in the DRC—and who knows: I may already be back there before the English edition of this book is published. I want to establish a structure within civil society that will promote the organization of the population—one that will help them to intensify their vigilance, not stand idly by.

I for my part rejoice and am hopeful, because the valiant UDPS fighters, as well as a huge number of human rights groups, civil society organizations, and social movements, remain alert, continuing their mission to question leaders and push them to take action for the well-being of the vast majority of the population. Whenever the new president of the republic is seen in Kinshasa, or when he travels to any of the DRC's provinces, both UDPS militants and the general population call out to him constantly to remind him of this. It is essentially a warning to both the new authorities and the party leaders, showing that the rank and file will not hesitate to punish those in power if they fail to serve the people well.

CONTACT INFORMATION

This book by Emmanuel Mbolela aims, among other things, to stimulate debate, and to spread the word about the Baobab guesthouse for migrant women. We therefore welcome your feedback, as well as invitations for readings and discussions with the author, including from universities, schools, and other educational institutions.

Please contact:

Alexander Behr

alexander.behr@univie.ac.at

LIST OF ABBREVIATIONS

ADESCAM   Association de développement et de sensibilisation
   des Camerounais migrants au Maghreb [Association for the
   Development and Sensitization of Cameroonian Migrants in the
   Maghreb]

AEI   Afrique-Europe-Interact

AFDL   Alliance des forces démocratiques pour la libération du Congo-
   Zaïre [Alliance of Democratic Forces for the Liberation of Congo-
   Zaire]

AFVIC   Association des amis et familles des victimes de l'immigration
   clandestine [Association of Friends and Families of Victims of Illegal
   Immigration]

AMDII   Association marocaine des droits humains [Moroccan
   Association for Human Rights]

AME   Association malienne des expulsés [Malian Association for
   Deportees]

ARCOM   Association de réfugiés et demandeurs d'asile congolais au
   Maroc [Association of Congolese Refugees and Asylum Seekers in
   Morocco]

ASD   Alliance pour la sauvegarde du dialogue inter-congolais [Alliance
   for the Protection of the Inter-Congolese Dialogue]

ATTAC   Association pour la taxation des transactions financières

et l'aide aux citoyens [Association for the Taxation of Financial
Transactions and Aid to Citizens]

COFESVIM   Comité des femmes et enfants subsahariens victimes de
l'immigration clandestine [Feminist Committee of Victims of Illegal
Immigration]

CNS   Conférence nationale souveraine [Sovereign National Conference]

DIC   Dialogue inter-Congolais [Inter-Congolese Dialogue]

DRC [RDC]   Democratic Republic of the Congo [République
démocratique du Congo]

CFA franc   Franc de la Communauté Financière Africaine—currency
of the West African economic and currency union, i.e., of Benin,
Burkina Faso, Côte d'Ivoire, Guinea-Bissau, Mali, Niger, Senegal,
and Togo

Frontex   European Agency for the Management of Operational
Cooperation at the External Borders of the Member States of the
European Union

GADEM   Groupe antiraciste d'accompagnement et de défense des
étrangers et migrants [Antiracist Group for Support and Defense of
Foreigners and Migrants]

IOM   International Organization for Migration

LOS   Stichting Landelijk Ongedocumenteerden Steunpunt [Dutch
Support Center for Undocumented Migrants]

MLC   Mouvement de libération du Congo [Movement for the Liberation
of the Congo]

MPR   Mouvement populaire de la révolution [Popular Movement of the
Liberation—sole political party of Congo/Zaire, 1967–1997]

NGO   Nongovernmental organization

PJD   Parti de la justice et du développement [Justice and Development
Party, Morocco]

RCD   Rassemblement congolais pour la démocratie [Rally for
Congolese Democracy]

RCD-N   Rassemblement congolais pour la démocratie [National Rally
for Congolese Democracy]

SOC   Sindicato de obreros del campo [Union of Workers of the Field—
Andalusian agricultural workers' union]

UAF   Universitair Asiel Fonds [Foundation for Refugee Students]

UDPS   Union pour la démocratie et le progrès social [Union for
    Democracy and Social Progress]

UNDP   United Nations Development Programme

UNHCR   United Nations High Commissioner for Refugees

UNICEF   United Nations Children's Fund

ACKNOWLEDGMENTS

The idea of writing a book was on my mind for a long time before I came to the Netherlands. I thought a lot about how I might convey the fate of migrants to a wider audience. My initial intention was just to write a report about the activities of ARCOM and circulate this among the social move-ments and networks. I told Dr. Anad-ler Kalunji about my idea. He advised me to start writing a book straightaway. A report, he said, was too infor-mal, and not enough people would take notice of it.

The writing process was not easy for me. I had to keep setting the book aside for long periods, because I was still deeply affected by the things I was writing about. In remembering, I relived it all again. Often, I would find myself weeping as I wrote. I felt great pain; sometimes also remorse and guilt.

I completed my manuscript in the Netherlands. Annie and Didier François from Paris, who let me stay with them during the "Des Ponts, Pas Des Murs" summit, agreed to read it and send me their suggested correc-tions. I am very grateful to them for this.

It was only because the publication of the first edition of the book was postponed that I was able to write the seventh and final chapter. I was therefore able also to put into writing my experiences in Europe, and to share them with readers.

I would not have succeeded in finishing this book without the help of a great many friends from the network Afrique-Europe-Interact. I would like to extend my heartfelt thanks to Olaf Bernau, who invested many hours in reading the manuscript and gave me very sound and pertinent advice. His wise remarks will also help me fulfill the political tasks that still lie ahead of me. Without the efforts of Alexander Behr, the manuscript of this book would probably still be sitting in the drawer of my desk. He was the one who, on first reading it, expressed an interest in getting it published, looked for a publisher, and translated it into German. I also acknowledge the work of François Bouchardeau as well as Isabelle Stettler, who invested a great deal of time in correcting the French version. I would also like to express my gratitude to Valentina Malli and Barbara Vecchio, who translated the book to Italian for the "Agenzia X" edition, and Charlotte Collins, who brought my words to life in English. I must also thank Vincent de Jong, whose notes on the content were also extremely helpful to me. Finally, I would like to thank Jean Ziegler with all my heart. Ziegler, who is known worldwide as a member of the UN Human Rights Council and as a public intellectual, wrote a great foreword for the German edition of the book and supported me without ceasing, emphasizing the importance of my work many times in his lectures and interviews.

This book is dedicated to all my comrades in arms from Mbuji-Mayi who were killed by police bullets in the fight for our rights, for democracy and freedom; to all the friends with whom I shared my journey, and the time in Morocco; and to my close companion and brother Mutombo Mukadi. He died very suddenly while I was living in Morocco. I never had the chance to pay my last respects.

A Note About the Author

Emmanuel Mbolela is an author, an activist, and a refugee. He was born in the Democratic Republic of the Congo and studied economics in Mbuji-Mayi. In 2002, he was arrested because of his political engagement. After his release, he was forced to emigrate and embarked upon a six-year odyssey through West Africa, the Sahara, and Morocco. In 2008, he was granted asylum in the Netherlands. He originally published *Refugee* in German in 2014.

A Note About the Translator

Charlotte Collins translates literary fiction and plays from the German. She was awarded the Helen and Kurt Wolff Translator's Prize in 2017 for *A Whole Life*, by the Austrian author Robert Seethaler, which was also shortlisted for the Man Booker International Prize. Her other translations include Seethaler's *The Tobacconist*, *Homeland*, by Walter Kempowski, *The End of Loneliness*, by Benedict Wells, and Nino Haratischwili's *The Eighth Life* (cotranslated with Ruth Martin).